KW-226-288

THE COTSWOLDS
Some Stories of its Villages & Churches

Other books by
ERIC R. DELDERFIELD

* The Cotswold Countryside and its Characters
* Church Furniture
* Introduction to Inn Signs
* British Inn Signs and their Stories
* West Country Historic Houses and Their Families
Exmoor Wanderings
Fascinating Facts and Figures of the Bible
North Devon Story

and other titles

* Published by David & Charles Ltd., Newton Abbot, Devon

THIRD EDITION

The COTSWOLDS

Some Stories of the Villages and Churches

by

ERIC R. DELDERFIELD

With 25 Photographs by the Author

Published by E.R.D. Publications Ltd., Exmouth, England.

THE COTSWOLDS

Some Stories of the lovely Villages and Churches

First Published: March, 1961
Reprinted: June, 1961, and February, 1962
Second Edition: January, 1965
Third Edition, Revised and Enlarged: March, 1969

900345 02 0

Printed in Great Britain by
Sawtells of Sherborne Limited, Dorset

CONTENTS

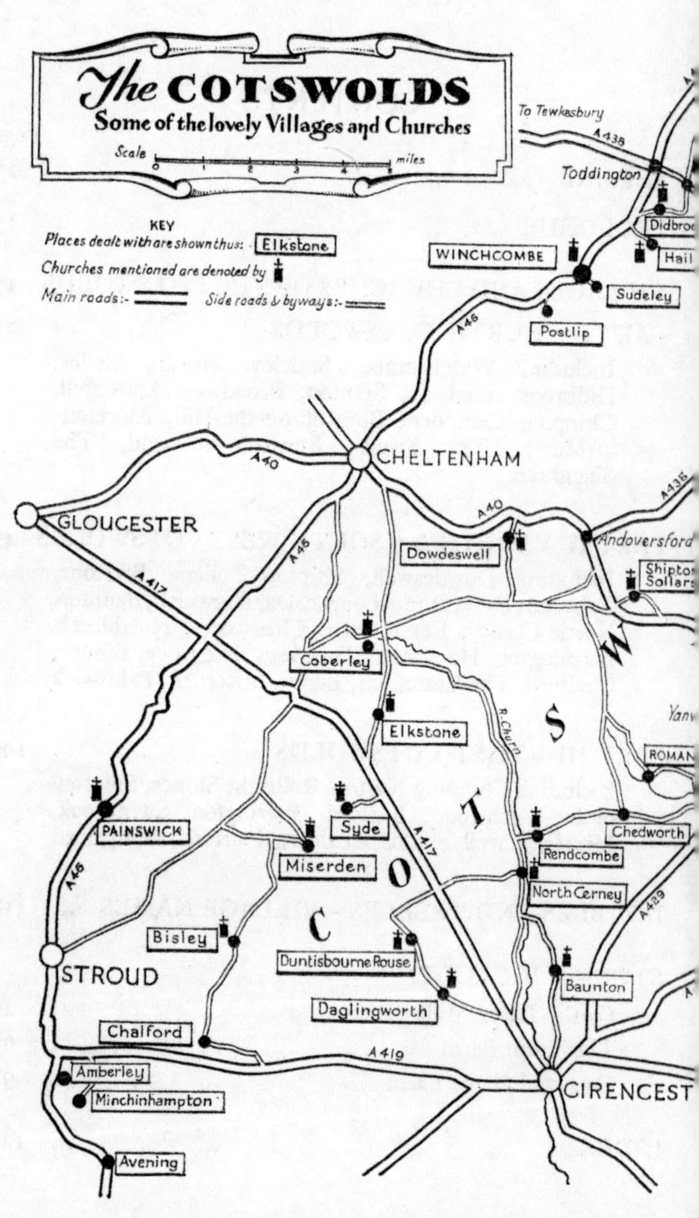
The COTSWOLDS
Some of the lovely Villages and Churches
Scale
0
1
2
3
4
5
miles
KEY
Places dealt with are shown thus: Elkstone
Churches mentioned are denoted by
Main roads:-
Side roads & byways:-
To Tewkesbury
A438
Toddington
Didbrook
Hail
WINCHCOMBE
Sudeley
Postlip
A46
CHELTENHAM
A40
GLOUCESTER
A40
A435
Andoversford
Dowdeswell
Shipton Sollars
A46
A417
Coberley
Elkstone
R. Churn
Yanw
ROMAN
Syde
Miserden
PAINSWICK
A417
Chedworth
Rendcombe
North Cerney
A429
A46
Bisley
Duntisbourne Rouse
Baunton
STROUD
Daglingworth
Chalford
A419
Amberley
Minchinhampton
CIRENCEST
Avening
C O T S W

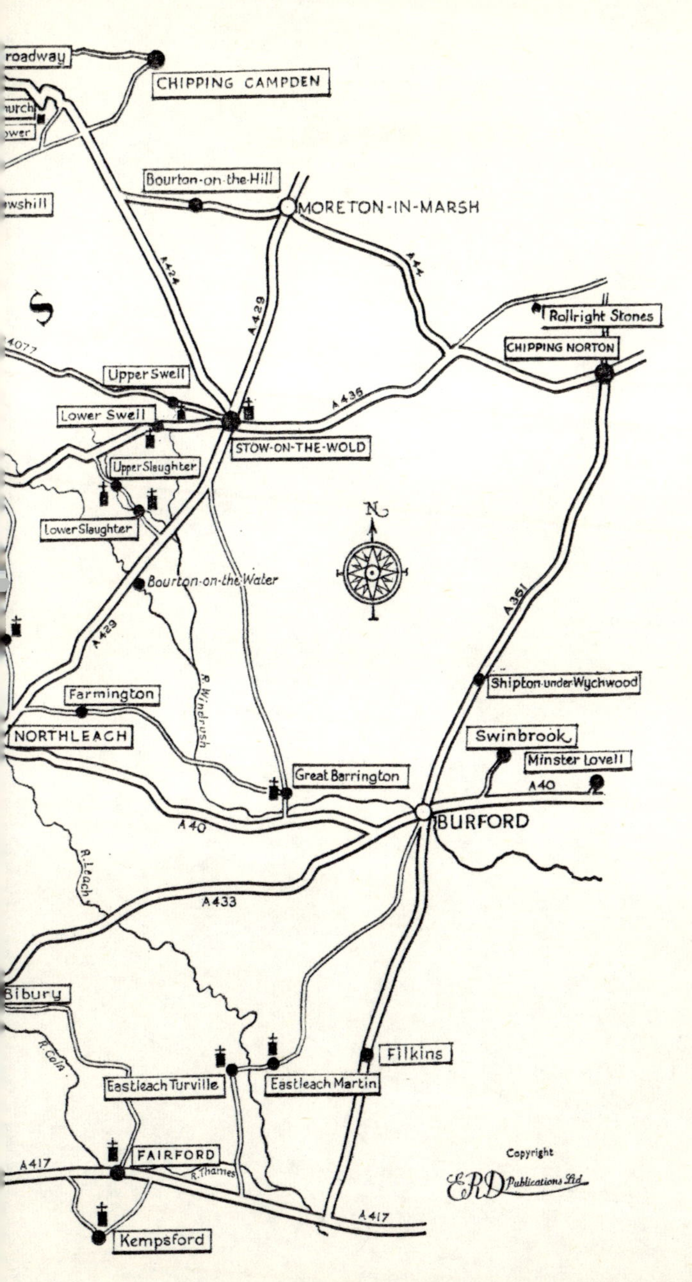

roadway
CHIPPING CAMPDEN
hurch
ower
Bourton-on-the-Hill
MORETON-IN-MARSH
wshill
A424
A429
A44
Rollright Stones
CHIPPING NORTON
A077
Upper Swell
A436
Lower Swell
STOW-ON-THE-WOLD
Upper Slaughter
Lower Slaughter
N
Bourton-on-the-Water
A351
A429
R. Windrush
Farmington
Shipton-under-Wychwood
NORTHLEACH
Swinbrook
Minster Lovell
Great Barrington
A40
A40
BURFORD
R. Leach
A433
Bibury
R. Coln
Filkins
Eastleach Turville
Eastleach Martin
FAIRFORD
A417
R. Thames
A417
Kempsford
Copyright
ERD Publications Ltd

ILLUSTRATIONS

PREFACE

THIS is a book about the COTSWOLDS – no particular part, no particular subject. Just stories about villages, churches and people, past and present. There is no set plan, no set route – which will explain why many villages and all the larger towns have been omitted.

The reason for this is three-fold. Firstly, many people go to the Cotswolds and prefer to wander. Part of the charm of the area is that there is something beautiful and something interesting in the smallest village, which is often missed in following a set itinerary. Secondly, an attempt to include everything would make a massive volume, or alternatively many stories would have to be omitted. Finally, every effort has been made to avoid making this 'just another guide book'.

In a review of a similar book on another part of the country a few years ago, the reviewer said: "This is a book one can pick up at odd times or keep by the bedside. There is something of interest on every page to catch the eye". If the same can be said of this book and at the same time bring more people to love the Cotswolds, its villages and churches, then I shall have achieved all I have set out to do.

The text has been so arranged that the places mentioned fall very roughly into three areas – north, south and south-west and east. This has been done for convenience and is not necessarily geographically correct.

This is the third edition and there have been six printings since the book was first published in 1961. I have taken the opportunity to bring certain items up-to-date, make some additions and change some of the pictures.

The preceding map has been designed to show the approximate position of each place in relation to the larger villages and towns.

E. R. DELDERFIELD.

Penshurst, Exmouth, Devon.

PROLOGUE

If visitors will go up to the North Cotswolds between the Dickler and the Evenlode Valleys and there, 800 ft above sea level, look down on the village of Stow-on-the-Wold, they may, if their imagination is keen enough, catch glimpses of an endless cavalcade – a Cavalcade of History.

Along the line that the modern highway A429 follows today, the Roman Legions are on the march from Cirencester to Lincoln; well-fed monks tell their beads as they walk along; wealthy wool merchants astride their high-stepping horses and following on thousand upon thousand of Cotswold sheep move slowly along, tended by Gloucestershire shepherds. Princes and courtiers pass by in a colourful parade; hucksters, travelling acrobats and characters from Chaucer's Tales; cavaliers gallop by, pursued by Cromwell's Ironsides; and from time to time, a hard-pressed nearly spent horse with its rider carrying news of national rejoicing or perhaps tidings of a battle fought at Tewkesbury's 'Bloody Meadow' or Naseby.

The cavalcade is endless and but part of the story of England – a glittering procession that has passed and re-passed the Roman roads of the Cotswolds over the centuries. The Cotswolds, rich in history, fortunate in churches and architecture, agriculturally wealthy, clean and peaceful is England at its best.

VILLAGES AND CHURCHES OF THE COTSWOLDS

THE villages and churches of the Cotswolds are synonymous. Wherever men settled they built a church, which not only catered for their spiritual needs but also became the centre of the community life of the village. The history of every village and township has, therefore, been created round the church and what a fascinating history it is.

'As sure as God is in Gloucestershire' was a well-known saying in medieval times, and it was thought to have referred to the traditional relic of the Blood of Christ at Hailes Abbey. The saying could just as well have been a reference to the number of churches and religious institutions in the county. There were four great abbeys - St Peter's, Gloucester (now the Cathedral), Cirencester, Winchcombe and Hailes - the latter particularly, attracting many thousands of pilgrims every year. There were nunneries at Withington, Daglingworth and Pinbury: priories at Burford, Broadway and Lechlade, to name just a few. In addition, almost every hamlet had its Norman church whilst those in the towns were of a magnificence to compare with any in the land.

There has not been a great deal of change. Today, almost every road leads to an ancient church, which more than likely is built on the site of an earlier one. Most of them are of architectural interest and all have an interesting story.

The chapel at POSTLIP for instance, was built by the lord of the manor because his tenants dreaded cut-throats and wandering robbers on the long dark road to Winchcombe, where then was situated the parish church.

HAILES ABBEY was founded by the brother of a king, as the result of a vow made during a storm at sea when he feared for his life.

STOW-ON-THE-WOLD church was once a temporary prison for Sir Jacob Astley and a thousand Royalist troops.

The church at LOWER SWELL is a church within a church.

The stone altar of WYCK RISSINGTON has had a chequered history, for it was altar, church paving stone and tombstone before it was restored to its present position.

At BURFORD 400 'Levellers' were imprisoned in the church in 1649 and indeed, three of their number were shot in the churchyard.

The chancel at SHIPTON SOLLARS is unique in being lower than the nave. So many people were buried in the nave that the floor rose above chancel level.

Cotswold churches are rich in Norman work and probably 75 per cent. of the present buildings stand on sites they occupied in those times.

A great number of our English churches were built in the twelfth and thirteenth centuries and to appreciate the magnitude of the work one has to realise that the population of England then totalled only three millions. Even with the modern resources that are at hand today, it would be an enormous if not an impossible task to emulate those men of long ago. Only a great love and an abounding faith, hand-in-hand with the pride of the craftsmen, made this supreme period of church building possible. It is a remarkable fact that when the new Guildford Cathedral was completed in 1962, it was the first cathedral to be built on a *new* site in this country for 500 years.

The famous Cotswold 'wool' churches mostly owe their grandeur to the piety and wealth of the merchants of the fourteenth, fifteenth and sixteenth centuries.

There are five churches in particular which are magnificent examples of Perpendicular architecture and all were either rebuilt or greatly embellished by patrons enriched by the wool trade. These fine notable 'wool' churches are Burford, Cirencester, Fairford, Northleach and Winchcombe. Numerous others all over the Cotswolds benefited to some degree from similar generosity.

In the following pages, some of the villages and the churches of the Cotswolds are mentioned. Just a few of the interesting stories are briefly told, but for every one mentioned probably three or four have been omitted.

NORTH COTSWOLDS

WINCHCOMBE

Winchcombe, midway between Cheltenham and Broadway, is a fascinating old English town which has a wealth of history. Once a Saxon walled city, an important Benedictine abbey was later built there. Tithes were contributed from thirty-three parishes which were widely scattered. By order of Henry VIII, the abbey was razed to the ground in the sixteenth century so thoroughly that no stone was left above another. In the Civil war period several skirmishes were fought around the town and indeed Sudeley Castle nearby was put to siege more than once.

Perhaps one of Winchcombe's little-known claims to fame is that it was among the first places where tobacco was grown in this country. Despite many ruthless attempts by Parliament to stamp out the practise, the weed was cultivated there for some fifty years. The reasons for the prohibition were, of course, mainly political. It hindered the growth of the plantations in Bermuda and the Virginias, reduced customs revenue and spoiled the ground for other agricultural crops. The proclamation against the cultivation was signed by Queen Elizabeth, then in 1619 James I did something more than that – he levied a tax of 3d. in the pound, which gradually rose to 6s. 10d. in the pound.*

The people of Winchcombe did not lightly accept this interference, and proved so difficult that a troop of Life Guards was sent to the district. It is recorded, however, that

> '. . . The country did rise on them, above five or six hundred threatening to kill them, horse and man, so that they were constrained to depart.'

*In 1968 the tax on every pound of tobacco was 97/4d.

Eventually the planting of tobacco crops ceased, but there is still a field close to the town known as the 'Tobacco Close'.

Still to be seen on the archway of the George, which was originally a pilgrims' inn, are the initials 'R.K', Richard Kydermінster, who was Abbot of Winchcombe in the reign of Henry VII. Formerly a gallery ran right round the courtyard. Today, the old inn still lends grace and enchantment to the little township.

The winding main street is full of interest and there are a few surviving half doors to the houses, which are a reminder of the Gloucestershire saying that everyone who leaves a door open was born in Winchcombe. It is said that the large number of the original doors dated from a request by the Abbot of Hailes, that

> *'The good people of Winchcombe to leave their doors open as an encouragement to the numerous pilgrims passing through the town'.*

THE CHURCH

The building of Winchcombe church commenced in 1460, and it is one of the finest of the 'wool' churches. It is famous for its particularly grotesque gargoyles of which there are forty, ranging from a little man with wings and wearing a top hat, to an ugly teddy bear. The two-storied porch has a fine vaulted roof, and the upper room served as a Sunday school as late as the nineteenth century.

The lofty, slender and stately Perpendicular tower is surmounted by a massive and richly gilded weathercock, which belonged originally to the church of St Mary Redcliffe, Bristol. The age of this weathercock cannot be ascertained, but it was removed from Bristol when the church was restored in 1872. It is not generally appreciated that the proud bird is made of copper and is very large, measuring 6ft from beak to tail and 4ft 6in in height. It weighs three hundredweight.

The interior of the church is spacious and lofty. There are twenty-four clerestory windows in the nave, three richly carved screens and a canopied triple sedilia. There is also an ancient pillar almsbox hollowed out from a tree and provided with the usual three locks.

A rare possession is an altar-cloth, said to have been made by Catherine of Aragon, the first queen of Henry VIII. It is a coincidence that Catherine Parr, the last queen of the much married monarch, died in nearby Sudeley Castle.

The holes in the stonework round the west door of the church are said to have been made by bullets during the fighting in the Civil war.

SUDELEY CASTLE

Less than a mile off Winchcombe's main street is Sudeley Castle, which has seen so much of the history of England unfold. A rich cavalcade of kings, queens and princes have passed through its gateway. Soldiers have fought for possession and sieges and surrender took place in quick succession during the Civil War. It was finally destroyed by the troops of the Parliament. Lord Chandos, who owned it during that period, was fined £4,976, a tidy sum in those days, for his loyalty to Charles and when the castle was demolished in 1650, he was allowed a paltry £1,000 compensation to be deducted from his fine.

But the glory of Sudeley was in earlier days, when Catherine Parr, widow of Henry VIII, spent the last months of her life there. Her coffin lay in an unknown spot for 250 years, yet when it was discovered in 1782, her body was in a perfectly preserved state. Poor Catherine! She was the widow of Lord Brough when she was thirteen years of age. She was married again to eighty-year-old Lord Latimer and then became the wife of Henry VIII until his death. At last she was able to marry the man of her own choice, but he proved a rogue and a libertine, who was beheaded after thirty-three counts of treason had been levelled against him. Two future queens of England were also with Catherine Parr at Sudeley, the Princess Elizabeth and Lady Jane Grey. Catherine herself died at the age of thirty-six, giving birth to a daughter.*

Today, visitors may inspect the castle, the lovely chapel and gardens on certain days, which are advertised locally.

POSTLIP HALL

From the main Cheltenham/Winchcombe road, a long drive leads to Postlip Hall, a twelfth-century building with Tudor additions, which was originally the centre of a manor of 4,000 acres. It is a magnificent house containing some seventy rooms and has the distinction of being the only surviving manor house with two chapels.

The Catholic chapel was built by William de Solers, one of the Conqueror's followers, because his tenants feared the long dark road to the parish church at Winchcombe. When the estate changed hands a few years ago, one of the conditions operating was that the owner of the Hall be responsible for the exterior of the building and the Roman Catholics for the inside. The Protestant chapel is situated inside the house.

On the magnificent tithe barn close by is an effigy of the proud Norman baron, Sir William de Postlip.

THE PAPER MILLS

The Cotswold villages are full of surprises and tucked away, on the outskirts of the North Cotswolds is Postlip paper mill which has been flourishing for about 200 years. Records

* *The story appears in Cotswold Countryside and its Characters*

show that there was a flour mill on the same site in Saxon times but certainly since 1789, and probably before, the mill in this beautiful rural setting has been making fine papers. The concern has been in the ownership of the same family since 1849 and it was about that date when steam power was installed. Prior to that, power was supplied by one of the largest water mills in the country. This, however, had its drawbacks, chief of which was the shortage of water in the summer months when work had to be abandoned.

The firm has taken considerable strides in the twentieth century and since the last war the mills have been modernised and expanded considerably, to serve the new industries, in particular filters for giant automobile and engine requirements. A small but interesting development too, is in the supply of specialised filter papers made entirely from glass fibre, which is used largely for the removal of radio-active particles to purify the air in nuclear establishments. Strange that all this is taking place in the quiet Cotswold countryside.

HAILES ABBEY

The grandeur that was Hailes belonged to the thirteenth century, for today only a few crumbling walls remain of what was for 300 years, the most popular place of pilgrimage in the West Country.

The abbey was founded by Richard, brother of Henry III, as the result of a vow made in 1242 when he thought the vessel in which he was returning from the Continent was about to be wrecked in a great storm. He did, however, land safely in the Scilly Isles and so returned to England to fulfil his vow on a magnificent scale and at a cost of ten thousand marks. It was a sum he could well afford for he was the richest man in the kingdom. The king and queen, bishops, abbots, nobles and knights attended the lavish consecration ceremony. The abbey with its twenty monks and ten lay brothers, already had claims to fame.

But further glory was added when the sacred relics, a piece of the true cross and a phial of the blood of Christ, came into its possession. They were placed in an elaborate sacred shrine of silver and what was important, the relics carried with them a certificate of authenticity given by the Patriarch of Jerusalem. The fame of the abbey spread far and wide; thousands of pious pilgrims made the journey to Gloucestershire and it was said that "God daily sheweth miracles through the virtues of the Holy Relics". These manifestations, however, were not accepted by all and soon there were those blasphemers who whispered that the relic was nothing more than the blood of a duck. This story gained ground and the stream of pilgrims began to slacken, but the Pope came to the rescue by offering Indulgences to all who made the pilgrimage to Hailes, so the Abbey quickly regained its prestige and glory.

The dissolution of the monastery followed some half a century later, when the relics were confiscated and the shrine smashed. The "blood" was analysed and found to contain nothing more than honey, coloured with saffron, a concoction which had been renewed annually. One can imagine the sardonic humour of Henry VIII, who had the fraud publicly burnt at Paul's Cross, London, in 1539. The abbey then became the property of Thomas Seymour, of nearby Sudeley Castle, who promptly demolished it.

Today one may still see the ruins of this once glorious pile and excavations are still going on. The planting of conifers where the nave piers once stood, give an idea of the size and scale of the chuch as it was. It is particularly interesting in the light of the story, to see the various spots marked. Richard, the founder, was buried close to the high altar, at least his body was. His heart was interred with the remains of his fourth wife in an Oxford church. One can see where the sacred shrine of the "holy blood" was gazed upon with reverence by pilgrims from far and near, all those centuries ago. Just behind the shrine, the son of the founder was buried in 1271. In this quiet corner of the Gloucestershire countryside, the story of Hailes Abbey comes to life.

Close by an interesting little museum has been built and some of the items saved from the wreckage of 500 years ago are on display. The museum is open all the year round.

HAILES CHURCH

A portion of the spoils of the abbey were used in embellishing the church close by. Some encaustic tiles and a great many heraldic tiles were used. There are some wall paintings and a fine black and white timber roof.

Variation in the spelling of Hailes, leads to much confusion. There is a Hailes street in Winchcombe; the abbey ruin is fingerposted *Hayles* and documents in the museum spell it as Heyles. Seventeenth-century tombs in the church favour the former spelling.

Hailes is just off the main Cheltenham/Broadway A46 road, beyond Winchcombe.

DIDBROOK

Tucked away on the country road between Stanway and Hailes, is the diminutive village of Didbrook. The door of the little church still bears marks of the fighting that ensued when the Yorkists were rounding up fugitives after the battle of Tewkesbury. Some poor wretches got into the church safely and assumed, as was the custom in those days, that they had found sanctuary. The ferocity of the Wars of the Roses and particularly after this battle, was quite alarming even for those days, and the Yorkists hot on the heels of their quarry followed them into the church and slaughtered them. Normally the building would have been re-consecrated but it was instead demolished and rebuilt in 1475. The church is unusual, in that it has no south or north door, only the battle-scarred west door.

STANWAY

Stanway is a twin village to Stanton and is separated by a mile of lovely parkland, through which the road meanders. The ancient tithe barn is one of the oldest in England and its huge buttresses and massive timbers have been in place for over 600 years.

Stanway House in the centre of the village, has a handsome gateway often incorrectly attributed to Inigo Jones. On the lawn is a fine tulip tree, under which Edward VII once had tea.

In the village lived the celebrated Doctor Thomas Dover, who was privateer captain (to all intents and purposes a pirate). In 1708, he sacked Guayaquil in Peru and became wealthy. He cured his ship's crew of the plague and was the inventor of Dover Powders, an 18th century sedative which is used to this day. Whilst most of his adventurous life is forgotten, to him will go the credit always for rescuing Alexander Selkirk from the island of Juan Fernandez. The story formed the basis of Defoe's immortal *Robinson Crusoe*. Dover died in 1742, a respected physician, and was buried in the vault of a friend in the village churchyard. It was Dover's grandfather, Robert, who founded the Cotswold Games, known as the 'Olympicks' as a festival of sport in 1604. The Games attracted people from hundreds of miles away and were held annually in Whit week at Dover's Hill, a natural amphitheatre, near Chipping Campden. Dover staged the event for nearly forty consecutive years. He died in 1652, and was buried at Barton-on-the-Heath.

STANTON

The by-road which leads to Stanton from the main road is an avenue flanked by elm, oak and chestnut trees and is a fitting approach to the kind of village that most of us imagine to be the 'old England' of days gone by. The houses are of Tudor style, built of stone with Cotswold tiled roofs of that lovely hue and dignity which comes with age. Each cottage has its colourful garden and the village Cross with its twelfth century base and the church tower rising from the centre of the village, make a delightful scene.

Stanton, however, is more than a pretty village. It is a model, thanks to the generosity of a former lord of the manor, Mr. Philip Scott (afterwards Sir Philip), who purchased the property in 1906. At that time most of the buildings in the village were in a dilapidated condition. The new owner commenced restoration immediately. A waterworks with its reservoir holding a million gallons was built; sewerage works were installed; farm houses, cottages and other buildings repaired and completely modernised, and trees were planted. In 1910, a public bathing pool was built just outside the village, but operations virtually ceased during the first World War. With the coming of peace, the work recommenced. A new heating apparatus was installed in the church, the post office was enlarged and electric light brought to the community.

None of this has affected the charm of Stanton and one imagines that the village may well remain unique in this respect, for the day of wealthy landlords seems to be over.

By a weird geographical quirk and the fact that the village is on the county border, the postal address of Stanton is Worcestershire, yet it is in Gloucestershire.

The church is more than 500 years old and has many points of interest, not the least the two pulpits; one was used for some 300 years before being replaced. It now stands in the church. It is a small wooden Gothic structure, warped and mutilated but still a valuable relic of medieval preaching, said to be dated about 1375. The pulpit in use today is of oak with fine panels and this too is famous in its way, for Charles Wesley preached one of his earliest sermons from it. Stanton's parson of that day being a University friend of Wesley.

There is a little room above the porch of the church, which serves as a tiny museum. The room is only seven feet square, with agricultural instruments and other items on display. The door opening on to the steps which lead to this chamber appears blocked by the second pew but the authorities have thoughtfully provided a removable back to the pew, which when swung back allows access to the door and the steps.

The rood and screen were the gift of Sir Philip Stott, in memory of his nineteen-year-old son, who died in 1915. The rood looks a little sombre and it is a pity it is not in the glory of medieval colour.

Close to the chancel is an ancient gravestone, which might have had an association with Stevenson's *Treasure Island* by the bold skull and crossbones incised upon it.

The church register has an illustrious name in its pages for in 1921, Major H. L Ismay was married to Miss Laura Kathleen Clegg of Wormington Grange nearby. In 1947 Lord Ismay retired after a lifelong army career and a particularly brilliant war record, and now resides at Wormington Grange, a mile from Stanton.

BROADWAY

Standing on the edge of the Cotswolds and at the commencement of the Vale of Evesham, Broadway needs no introduction for it is probably the best known of all English villages. That it has become a 'must' for visitors has naturally detracted from its charm, for during the summer months it is crowded with sightseers. But it is still beautiful with its neat buildings each with their mullioned windows, gables and stone slated or thatched roofs.

There is still a picturesque village green and by an ancient edict, a fair takes place there once a year. It is strange to hear the jarring note of the organs of the roundabouts and diesel engines, in such a setting – a far cry indeed from the old English fairs of long ago; we should be grateful it is only once a year. For all that, the fairs of long ago must have been fun when there were twenty-three inns in the village!

There are many attractive corners and byways and the rear of the houses and cottages are often more unspoilt than the front.

The Greatest Book Collector

The large country house, some two miles from the village, was occupied in the eighteenth century by Sir Thomas Phillipps, one of the greatest collectors of books and manuscripts the world has ever known. His is an interesting story.

Even at Oxford, Phillipps had a passion for collecting, but when his father died he inherited a mansion, *Middle Hill*, with a considerable amount of money and from then on devoted his life to accumulating books and manuscripts. He purchased whole libraries and collections travelling all over Europe, outbidding all others in amassing not only books, but rare illuminated manuscripts. Some of them were exquisite works of art and had been executed for the Medici, for various Popes, for

Ferdinand and Isabella of Spain and many other monarchs. One item he particularly treasured was a thirteenth-century book of miniature paintings of Bible incidents. Other volumes were bound in metal and studded with gems. In ten years he spent £100,000 but he went on collecting for thirty years after that, and not surprisingly was continually in debt.

The twenty rooms of the mansion at Broadway became crammed from cellar to attic with books and manuscripts. When space could not be found for another volume he purchased Thirlestaine House, Cheltenham, which is now part of the Cheltenham Boys' College. The removal of his collection from one house to the other took two years but he was adding to his collection all the time. In 1872, when eighty years of age, he died and the conjecture as to what would happen to his vast collection in the event, was at last settled. Years before he had provisionally offered it to the British Museum if they would pay his debts, for more than once he was on the verge of bankruptcy. Bangor College could have had the collection but for a strange condition which prevented it – that no Roman Catholic should ever be allowed access to the books. In the end he left them all to his third daughter.

Many of the treasures were sold separately. Dr. Rosenbach, the famous American collector, paid more than £100,000 for some, and others were sold to the Berlin State Library and the Pierpont Morgan Library.

Fourteen years passed before the vast accumulation could be arranged for sale, and at last in 1886 Messrs. Sotheby & Co. held the first of the Phillipps' manuscript sales. The auctions went on at intervals over the next eighty years and something approaching half-a-million pounds was realised. In 1965, all that remained of the collection was sold to a firm of London booksellers.

Middle Hill remains today, still a fine house in a magnificent situation.

Broadway's Old Church

The church which served Broadway for centuries lies a mile or so from the village on the road that leads to Snowshill. Dedicated to a rare saint, St Eadburgha, who was a granddaughter of King Alfred, it dates from the twelfth century. Unfortunately, on the plea that the building was too far from the community, it was to all intents and purposes abandoned in 1832 and a new church was built close to the village.

Services are still held at intervals in the old church, which has a great deal of interest within its walls. There are Norman columns, a tub font which is probably pre-Norman; quaint and interesting memorials and a fine 'brass'.

There is an altar tomb to Sir Thomas Phillipps, who was buried in the churchyard. There is a fine carved oak panel depicting eight of the apostles and several quaintly lettered memorials. Every church once had its parish bier, though such items are now rare. There is one in this church still to be seen. It was presented in 1888.

Unfortunately the death-watch beetle is playing havoc with the roof timbers of St Eadburgha's, though efforts are being made to eradicate the pest.

Broadway Tower

Broadway's village street peters out and the road climbs steeply to Fish Hill, giving superb views of the surrounding countryside. At the summit (1,024ft) is the *Fish* inn and farther along the Stow road, are a pair of columns serving as a gateway to a by-road which leads to Broadway Tower. One hundred and sixty years ago the Countess of Coventry was curious to know whether the hill could be seen from her home near Worcester, whereupon her husband obligingly arranged for a beacon to be lit there, and when it was found that it could be seen quite clearly, ordered the tower to be built to act as a signal station to his residence. For centuries before, the spot was undoubtedly a fire beacon station, particularly during the Napoleonic wars. At a later date Sir Thomas Phillipps used it for his printing press.

The tower is open to the public in the summer months and for a small fee one can ascend it and on a clear day enjoy a panoramic view embracing thirteen counties.

SNOWSHILL AND ITS LOVELY MANOR

A mile or so off the main Cheltenham/Broadway road is the delightful village of Snowshill. Though typically Cotswold style, it is rescued from 'sameness' by an individual charm.

Here is Snowshill Manor, or as the 'locals' call it – 'Snawsille'. The building has as fascinating a history as one would expect of a building which had at different times three royal owners. It was formerly the property of Winchcombe Abbey; then in 1543 Henry VIII gave it to the last of his six queens, Catherine Parr, as part of her marriage settlement. Later it was owned by Edward VI, and then by Mary Tudor and her spouse, Philip of Spain.

By 1919 it was being used as a farmhouse and was showing years of sad neglect when Mr. Charles Wade, a scholar and architect, purchased the property and began to restore it. Unsightly outbuildings which had been thrown up at odd angles and corners in the yard, were pulled down and the new owner lavished care and thought on a series of delightful terraced gardens, which are now an outstanding feature of the place. Mr. Wade's hobby was collecting the weird and the wonderful. When he died, amassed in the rooms of this manor house was the most varied collection possible to imagine – so varied that it could be mistaken for an overspill of a dozen museums.

From a Japanese shrine and Tibetan scrolls to models of ships: from a fascinating collection of farm waggons to ingenious clocks and dolls' houses. In one corner is the tipstaff of a Bow Street runner and in another, a suit of medieval armour. Collections of musical instruments stand cheek by jowl with dozens of penny farthing bicycles. There is indeed something to interest all but a collector of shrunken heads!

The musical section is amazing. If one is interested in stringed instruments, then they can feast their eyes on harps, lutes, guitars, citterns, violins, dulcimers, lyres, a psaltery or even an ophicleide. If the preference is for wind instruments, then there is an extra wide choice, including—

serpents	horns	hautboys
bagpipes	flutes	flageolets
french horns	piccolos	ocarinas
cornets	clarinets	bugles
trumpets	pitch pipes	hurdy-gurdies.
bassoons	coaching horns	

Percussion is not forgotten for there are clavichords, drums, triangles, and kaffir pianos.

There are instruments from Russia, Italy, France, Ireland, Portugal, London and even Cheltenham Parish Church! Indeed a glorious profusion.

All the rooms carry odd names – "Seventh Heaven", "Seraphim", "Mermaid", "Top Gallant", etc. In the room on the left of the hall called "Admiral", is a collection of navigational instruments and objects of nautical flavour. Compasses, quadrants, octants, barometers and telescopes are mixed with traverse boards, bo'suns' pipes and an interesting figure of a sailor called a 'Dolly', a device formerly displayed in the windows of seamen's pawn shops.

An exhibit of considerable interest is a very large volume measuring some three feet by two feet, known as an *Antiphonal.* This is a manuscript book used for alternate singing in a monastery. Its size is accounted for by the fact that in order to be read in a dim light, everything was written exceptionally large. The words are on one side, the notation on the facing page. The covers of the book, which came from a fourteenth century abbey, are of stout board with heavy iron corners and clasps.

The "Great Garret" is known as the room of a hundred wheels, though there are many more than a hundred, for there is a fine collection of early bicycles from models on which both wheels were fixed to "penny farthings" and even one with a fifty-two inch driving wheel. On a shelf surrounding this room is a superb series of farm waggons, made to a scale of 1½ inches to a foot, showing what is not often appreciated, the wide difference in the waggon styles of the English counties.

Across the small courtyard from the main house is a smaller dwelling, where Mr. Wade lived in his later years. This is as he left it and just as packed with collections as the larger building. He preferred the medieval way of life and was not content with normal stairs, so he built a tiny turret stairway to his bedroom. The workshop, just as he left it, would be a joy to any "do-it-yourself" enthusiast, except that the only light was by candles and even those he made himself.

In a summer-house are some early *Merryweather* fire engines, very old but still mechanically perfect. One is of a type that was once the normal equipment of every church.

The gardens consist of a series of perfectly planned terraces, with queer pieces set here and there – an ancient clock, a religious figure, and so on.

This fascinating collection was presented by the owner to the National Trust in 1951, five years before his death.

It is a great pity that there is not more space and funds available, to arrange effectively the thousands of objects and to classify and make more easily identifiable the host of interesting things to be seen.

CHIPPING CAMPDEN

There is a delightful old-world dignity about Chipping Campden, which makes it probably the most pleasant little town in the Cotswolds. In the main street are houses and shops, no two of which are alike. There are old inns and the focal point a market hall, with its five semi-circular arches each side and two at either end, has graced the village since 1627.

Another wool town, Campden was fortunate in having several wealthy merchants residing there. The greatest benefactor was Sir Baptist Hicks, who became the first Lord Campden. He was so rich that he was able to lend money to the king. He built the great manor house, which was close by the church. Unfortunately it was destroyed during the Civil war. The gateways and quaint pavilions, however, still remain to show us something of the scale of the old mansion in its heyday. A row of almshouses close by were also provided by Sir Baptist.

In the main street is one of the finest examples of fourteenth century domestic architecture to be found in the Cotswolds, or even farther afield. It is Grevel House, home of another London merchant, William Grevel, who died in 1401. He left money for the rebuilding and enlargement of the church, in which he was buried.

Here, a fantastic experiment took place in the nineteenth century, when the Guild and School of Handicrafts moved there from Toynbee Hall in the East End of London. The scheme was the inspiration of such men as Burne-Jones, William Morris and Ruskin.

Campden is a place in which to wander. At every turn there is something of beauty and interest. The houses with their canopied doorways and oriel windows, the smaller ones with their half doors opening on to the street, the Cotswold stone glowing with a sun drenched warmth that is apparent on even the dullest day. In a side street is a seventeenth century silk mill. Then there is the glorious church.

A mile or so away is Dover's Hill, a natural amphitheatre, where annually for half a century the celebrated games were held every Whit week, when everything from fencing to shin kicking and horse racing took place and often 500 prizes were awarded.

BOURTON-ON-THE-HILL

Close to Moreton is the pretty little village of Bourton-on-the-Hill, actually sitting as it were on the hill. Here are attractive cottages, an inn and the church, but there is little of interest in that building. The font was buried presumably to save it at the time of the Reformation. It was later recovered and cut to fit into one of the pillars. In 1894 it was placed in its present position. Also preserved there, are standard Winchester bushel and peck measures. Made of bell metal, they were ordered by the magistrates in 1816. They were then as a result of a decree by Elizabeth I the standard of the whole county, and used in disputes concerning corn rents and tithes. The measures were recovered and placed in the church in 1931.

MORETON-IN-MARSH

Moreton-in-Marsh, 5 miles north of Stow, is a pleasant little town, almost wholly built on each side of its wide main street. The name is believed to have come from Moreton-in-Marches, the word here meaning borders, for it is situated on the borders of three counties.

The church is not outstanding, but a rarity is the old lock-up which stands in the centre of the main street. The bell in the curfew tower is the original, which tolled up to about 100 years ago.

During the war there was a large R.A.F. camp on the outskirts of the town and the buildings now serve as a training establishment for the National Fire Service. At the White Hart hotel Charles I is said to have stayed one night in 1644. The handsome sign of the Redesdale Arms hotel is worth a glance. The Redesdales had a family home nearby at Batsford, where there was a famous collection of trees and plants.

A SCHOOL BRINGS NOSTALGIC MEMORIES

A school, rather a handsome one at that, was opened in the tiny village of Evenlode in 1844. For 122 years it played its part in catering for the children of a scattered community. In 1966, however, only about a dozen pupils remained and they were transferred to Moreton-in-Marsh, and the school closed.

At this time Mrs. Joan Cope was searching for suitable premises in which to mount a permanent exhibition of children's toys and games. The school became available at the right time and she moved in. Today, as a result an excellent little museum is open to the public in the summer months. Some will enjoy this for the nostalgia it will surely bring with it, others will become fascinated and the children will adore it.

Here gathered together by this lady, whose life-long hobby has been the collecting of toys, are items that most of us have long forgotten. By far the most numerous section are the dolls, for there are dozens of them. All sorts and sizes, beautiful and plain, and yes, even historical. The rarest is a pair of Queen Anne dolls in a small case. They are nearly 300 years old. Another was once the plaything of the sister of King Alfonso XIII of Spain. Quite special, it is a French doll dressed in Spanish costume, complete with a tambourine and a fan, which she holds in her hands. Unusual too, are the nun dolls, a type which was once a favourite on the continent. Some of these little ladies are complete to their rosary and diminutive prayer books. The dolls are of varied periods and from many countries, and together they make an entrancing display.

Most people have at some time played the card game of 'Happy Families' but never in the number of varieties in which this ageless party game is to be found at Evenlode. Another card game, popular at the time of the Suffragette troubles was known as 'Panko' after the Pankhursts). Cartoons on the cards were by E. T. Reed of *Punch* and the members of this particular 'family' included Chamberlain, Asquith, Balfour and Churchill. Other packs of cards have Shakespearian characters and eminent artists figure on others. A set of implements which formed the old game of Spillikens, are modelled from ivory, which reveal superb craftsmanship.

There are some of the earliest playthings which will never again be purchased for 1d. and, of course, no such collection would be complete without the miniature fully furnished Victorian drawing-room.

Much of Mrs. Cope's collection has been handed down through generations of her family. Items have been passed on to her by visitors, who feel happy that a toy that has given them years of pleasure should be preserved with care. Some were found in the walls of an ancient inn at Chipping Norton and these included a Napoleonic wooden soldier.

So the collection grows. Wherever the items come from they are assuredly still giving great pleasure and evoke memories to all who see them.

UPPER AND LOWER SWELL

One of the intriguing things about Cotswold villages, is the several pairs of villages each within a stone's throw of each other and each usually possessing a church.

Upper and Lower Swell are typical. The latter is quite delightful and it is believed that the name was derived from a medieval well, still marked as 'Our Lady's Well'. Generations of Cotswolds men have reduced it to S-well.

The church is of Norman origin and has many features of the period remaining, including the 800-year-old chancel arch. Formerly the church comprised a chancel and nave only but when it was rebuilt in the 1850's, a completely new church was built, utilising one wall of the old one. The old fabric was relegated as a south aisle and organ chamber.

Yet another interesting story about Lower Swell is that when the ground was being cleared for the new church, enormous deposits of red ash were discovered. Examined by experts it was found to be the residue of human cremation. Mixed with the dust were some Roman relics and experts consider that the original Saxon church had been built upon the site of a Roman crematorium.

The church of St Mary at Upper Swell, a mile away, retains the original Norman ground plan of chancel and nave. There are some Early English windows and a fine timber roof.

Next to the church is a very fine and well preserved Tudor manor house.

STOW-ON-THE-WOLD

Stow-on-the-Wold stands 800 ft above sea level at a point on the Great Fosse way where seven main roads meet.

Today a quiet little town, it has had its moments of historical importance and has seen prosperous periods to compare with any town twenty times its size. In the fourteenth and fifteenth century, it was the centre of the thriving wool trade and for hundreds of years its sheep fairs attracted trade from all parts of England and even from abroad.

In the seventeenth century, a journalist and novelist named Foe, who had served in Monmouth's Army during the abortive revolution, recorded that often 20,000 sheep were offered for sale in Stow's market place. This man, who changed his name to Defoe, was a prolific writer on a variety of subjects and published more than 250 items. He won everlasting fame with his *Robinson Crusoe* written in 1719.

The fine market square with some outstanding trees, is unusual for a Cotswold town. Something of its history may be gleaned from the old inns which flank the town centre.

The last important engagement of the first Civil War was fought at Stow on March 21st, 1646. Royalist troops under the command of the aged Sir Jacob Astley were defeated by Parliamentary troops. Sir Jacob with a thousand other prisoners was herded into Stow church. One can easily imagine the fine old warrior, a former sergeant-major who became a major-general, sitting on a drum and telling his captors:

Gentlemen, you may now sit down and play,
for you have done all your work, if ye not fall
out among yourselves.

It was the same old knight whose prayer before the battle of Newbury has become famous:—

Lord, I shall be verie busie this day:
I may forget Thee, but doe not Thou forget me.

Those who were imprisoned were the lucky ones. Many who were killed were buried where they died outside the town. Only one, Captain Keyte, has a tomb in Stow church.

There are records of a church at Stow in Saxon times but the fine church which now watches over the little town was built on a Norman foundation in the fifteenth century. The embattled tower is 80 ft in height and the walls are 5 ft thick. A large painting of the Crucifixion was the work of a Flemish artist, Gaspar de Craeyer, who was a pupil of Rubens. It was presented to the church in 1838, and until twenty years ago covered the beautiful stained glass east window. Visitors may see the picture to advantage by pressing a light switch, that has thoughtfully been provided.

THE SLAUGHTERS

An ugly name – but villages of beauty. That sums up the twin villages of Upper and Lower Slaughter. The latter with its clapper bridge of weathered stone, the chestnut trees, and pleasing little church, the old mill and the crystal clear stream, make this a dream village. The name comes from the lord of the manor in the twelfth century, 'de Sclotre', which generations of Cotswold folk have brought to 'Slaughter'.

The village is less than half-a-mile off the Stow/Northleach road.

Upper Slaughter, half-a-mile beyond, has an ancient church, which was modernised in the nineteenth century, also one of the finest seventeenth century manor houses in Gloucestershire.

SOUTH AND SOUTH-WEST COTSWOLDS

DOWDESWELL

Dowdeswell church near Cheltenham, has little remaining that is older than the seventeenth century but there is much of interest to remind the visitor of the heyday of the lord of the manor and the parson, for there are two galleries. That at the west end belonged to the lord of the manor and a much smaller one, in the north transept to the rector. Both had their private doors and staircases *outside* the church. It is strange in this small church to see the pews facing three ways. The chancel is some 3 ft above the level of the nave.

There is a 'brass' to a monk, which is dated about 1520, and a memorial brass plate just inside the sanctuary rail is interesting for its quaint spelling:—

> *Here Lyeth ye Body of*
> *John Crowther, Maister of Artes,*
> *Sometime Parson of this Parishe* (1623).

The Registers go back to 1554, and there is a story told that just after the first world war, two Americans came over specially to examine the records of the church. They excitedly examined the pages and of the 364 years of parish history so faithfully recorded, only one was missing – it was the page they required *to prove their title to a fortune!*

At the conclusion of the first war in 1918, rose trees were planted along the path in the churchyard to commemorate every man of the parish who had fallen. Their names were on a plaque beside each standard. Unfortunately, all the roses with but one exception have disappeared. It was a pleasant thought and a pity indeed that some re-planting cannot now be effected.

Adjacent to the church is an eight-gabled Elizabethan house, which is one of only three such dwellings known to exist.

Close by the church is Dowdeswell Court, a fine mansion set in extensive grounds. An Elizabethan mansion formerly occupied the site and at that time the village clustered round it.

The house is now the Chaplains' school of the Royal Air Force, which moved there in 1945 from Magdalene College, Cambridge, where it was formed in 1943 and housed during the war. The main work of the school consists in the conducting of moral leadership courses for all ranks of the Royal Navy and Royal Air Force. There is a resident staff of chaplains and a small but well furnished chapel in the house.

SHIPTON SOLLARS

The church of Shipton Sollars* lies on the left of the Cheltenham/Northleach road and is only a hundred yards or so from the main road. It adjoins a farmhouse and has a history of ruin and repair, and near ruin again. Not very many years ago it was very sympathetically restored and is well worth seeing for its fifteenth century trussed rafter roof. By the seventeenth century pulpit, is an hour glass, once used to time sermons. Judging by the amount of sand and its rate of fall, the sermons must have been marathons.

The chancel arch is Early English but probably the building is quite unique in Gloucestershire, for the fact that the chancel is several inches *lower* than the nave. This is due to the fact that no right of burial was attached to the churchyard at Shipton Sollars, so that many – too many – were buried within the nave, the level of which during the years was gradually raised, literally on the bones of the departed.

ELKSTONE

In this church, the most famous of all the Norman churches in Gloucestershire, is superb workmanship that has stood the test of 800 years. Even those who usually only glance at a

* There seem to be three accepted ways of the spelling. The old way was Solers and maps today show either Sollers, or Sollars.

church in passing, will find this one quite fascinating. It has the distinction too, of standing higher than any other church in the Cotswolds.

Today the tower is at the western end, but originally there was one which was either demolished or collapsed in the thirteenth century, and only a single low stage remains above the choir. The wonderful carving of the tympanum above the south doorway, represents Christ in Majesty surrounded by evangelical symbols. The left-hand of the central figure holds the Book of Judgment and the right is pronouncing the Blessing. The rich mouldings of beak heads and beaded chevrons are very fine.

The chancel is narrower than the nave and is divided to form a small choir and a perfect miniature sanctuary. The arch of the former is decorated with a pelleted hoodmould, terminated with dragons' heads, which in this form are rare.

Two windows towards the east end of the church are fine examples of Early English work and are responsible for the golden glow which suffuses the sanctuary on even the dullest day.

Just behind the pulpit is another delightful surprise, a newel stairway of twenty-eight tiny steps which leads to a large space over the chancel. This was at some time, presumably after the collapse of the tower, turned to a useful purpose and served as a dovecot complete with nesting holes.

There is a piscina in the sill of the south window and in the chancel is a small carved window head which came to light in 1959, when plaster covering the north door was removed. There is also a wall painting above the arch of the door.

This is one of the eight Cotswold churches which have representations of old musical instruments appearing in parts of the building. On two of the buttresses are gargoyles, lustily blowing a citole and a recorder. They are thought to be late 14th century work. The church is being cared for in an exemplary fashion and as renovations are carried out, so new and fascinating features come to light.

The registers, which date from 1592, are intact and though some of the earlier entries are indistinct, they have all been deciphered by a former rector. The earlier ones were written in latin and contain a wealth of parochial history. Typical of the human interest of these records are those of a Reverend William Prior, rector from 1682 to 1725. He must have been quite a character, as a few of his entries testify:—

1702. Jan. 17th was baptised Richard, the sonne of John Shill and Alice his wife. (I then whisped John that if he continued to be so great a strainger at Elston church I would no more baptise at his house).

1704. Dec. 6th was buried the stinking residue of William Gwylliams.

1707. June 19th was buried the bastard daughter of Mary Gwylliams, widdow, when I read in the church the seventh chapter of Proverbs.

1710. March 6th was buried the body of Susanna Townesen, a simple schismatic.

1718. Sept. 20th was buried Richard, one of the twin sons of John Bradly, slaine by a gunne shott off by a quick sighted marksman.

1724. Oct. 28th were married Joseph Shill and Mary Pool. (For future reference: he gave me what he gave to the sexton, a single miserable shilling!)

These entries are typical of the life centred round a country church of those days.

The house which was the rectory, a tudor building, stands in the corner of the churchyard, and the present vicarage, a Georgian building, is separated from the church by a cluster of holly and laurel bushes.

COBERLEY

Just three miles from Cheltenham on the main road to Cirencester, is a sign-post pointing to Coberley and a turn in the lane brings one to a charming group formed by the manor house and its attendant farm. Just behind them through an archway is the church. The farmyard is on one side of the church gate, the trim lawn of the house on the other. A delightful setting.

Though largely rebuilt the church is of ancient foundation. There are, however, several items of interest, particularly the tomb of Sir Thomas Berkeley, who fought at the battle of Crecy. His lady is beside him. She was the former wife of Sir Richard Whittington and mother of Sir Richard, three times lord mayor of London. The tomb also shows a small child with her pet dog at her feet.

An oval plaque in the sanctuary is a rare 'heart burial' monument, which is a reminder of a grim practice of the middle ages and even later. When someone of importance died abroad, they often bequeathed parts of their body to rest in different places. The body, therefore, was boiled in wine and separated. Thus the heart could be buried in one place, the flesh in another, and bones in another. This particular memorial in the form of an oval medallion, depicts a knight in armour, his mailed fists clutching a heart. It is believed to be that of Sir Giles de Berkeley, whose body was buried at Little Malvern and his heart at Coberley in 1295. His favourite charger was buried in the churchyard outside the chancel, only the thickness of the church wall dividing the animal from its master's heart. This is the only example of a 'heart burial' in the Cotswolds.

Close to Coberley are the Seven Springs, considered to be the source of the river Thames. Certainly it is the headwater furthest from the mouth of 'Father' Thames. The many claims of the true source were discussed in the House of Commons in

1937. On that occasion the Minister of Agriculture was asked if he was aware that on ordnance survey maps the source was shown at Thames Head, near Kemble. In view of the fact that the source known as Seven Springs was further from the estuary, the Minister was asked if he would undertake that in the next edition of the maps the correct source would be indicated. The member for Cirencester said, he was advised that the source of the Thames or Isis was the spring known as Thames Head, and that the leading authorities agreed that the name of the stream which rose at Seven Springs was the Churn. A further complication was introduced by suggesting that the real Thames was a stream known as the Willbrook, which rises in Wiltshire.

For the record, the Churn flows into the Thames at Cricklade and the Leach at Lechlade. Each have their devoted partisans, but the generally accepted view is that the source is considered that which is furthest from the mouth of the Thames, in which case Seven Springs at the juncture of A435 and A436 roads would appear to be indisputable.

SYDE

Syde church near Elkstone, is the centre of a group which is typical of the Cotswold hamlets and villages: the church, a former priest's dwelling and a farm, make a small and secluded group.

The main fabric of the church is Norman and there is a very unusual low 'saddleback' tower. There is no outside entrance to the basement, but steps give access direct to the ringing chamber, from where a ladder leads up to the belfry. There is a tie beam roof, plastered walls and plain oak box pews. One of which is outstanding and is discreetly shielded from the congregation.

Syde is the smallest parish in the county and there are fewer than forty souls within its area of 628 acres.

Mention is made elsewhere of the large number of marriages contracted at Hampnett church. Syde provides an example of the other extreme, for since 1600 only fifty-two marriages have been solemnised in the church, and recently the first for ten years took place.

The fine old tithe barn which faces the south door of the church has been closely associated with its long history. On the far side there is a portion which is thought to have been the priest's dwelling and it certainly has an ecclesiastical appearance. There are ancient and very attractively carved mullion windows and a fine old doorway, which are probably fourteenth century. There is too, a small window and aperture, which long ago housed a piscina. Today, the interior has been modernised but in an upper room an old bread oven still survives.

A few yards away is a manor house and in its forecourt is a well-head some six feet in diameter. The well, known to be very deep, is now covered by a massive stone.

A few hundred yards up the lane is another small house which is very ancient and could well have been the dwelling of a chantry priest attached to Syde church.

DUNTISBOURNE ROUSE

The miniature church of St Michael is certainly one of the most interesting of the smaller churches of the Cotswolds.

Its setting on a steep hillside overlooking the hills, farms, cottages and a stream below, is delightful. The church has a saddleback tower and the interior consists only of a chancel and nave. Little appears to have been altered since the seventeenth century. The chancel arch is twelfth century and there are five misericord seats which is unusual in so small a parish church.

They all have the same carved design of a lion's head surrounded by foliage. The nave has a black and white ceiling, and the walls are panelled with ancient pew ends.

Quite unique is the crypt beneath the chancel. Formerly it was approached by a flight of steps from the chancel but this entrance was blocked up long ago, and there is now a door leading from the churchyard. The crypt, about 9 ft by 15 ft, is as diminutive as the rest of the church. Part of the stairway to the chancel is still in being and at the eastern end, there is a deeply splayed Norman window. The roof has plain barrel vaulting. Crypts of this description are exceedingly rare in a small village church, although several are to be found in the larger Cotswold churches. The general use of such was to serve as a chapel for the celebration of masses for the dead and sometimes as confessionals. Following the Reformation, they were usually put to use as a charnel-house and sealed off. There are several grave slabs in the floor of this little building, which has fortunately been well preserved and cared for. Visitors are at liberty to enter and inspect for themselves.

There are altogether four villages bearing the name, Duntisbourne, but only two of them have churches.

DAGLINGWORTH

In the same area but closer to Cirencester is a church which has some carvings at least a thousand years old. They were discovered during building operations a hundred years ago. The panels are remarkably well preserved and are Saxon work of about the tenth century. Whilst perhaps the proportions leave a little to be desired, there is no mistaking the scenes which are most realistic and without doubt, that is more than will be said of some of the twentieth century efforts.

There are four carvings and they are now built into the walls of the church. They depict:—

South Wall: A Crucifixion scene with a Roman soldier standing each side of the central figure. One has a scourge and a spear, and the other a sponge on a stick and a bucket.

North Wall: (1) St. Peter clasping the key of heaven in one hand and a book in the other.

(2) Christ enthroned.

(3) A Crucifixion. (Christ wears a beard and a moustache).

Also unusual in this church are the curious brass memorial plates, set in to the floor of the porch. One of them, dated 1638, reads:—

"The dissection and distribution of Jiles Hancox who earth bequeathe to earth, to heaven his soule, to friends his love, to the poore a five pound dole".

Near the road, in the garden of a private house, is a remarkable dovecote with 550 nesting boxes. The revolving ladder for inspecting the holes, still exists.

In 1959, the Daglingworth Estate, comprising some 1,250 acres, was purchased by the Duchy of Cornwall, revenue from which in part is for the benefit of the Prince of Wales.

BAUNTON

In medieval days, St Christopher was a much loved saint. Just to look upon his image averted danger and ill luck, and he became a favourite figure of the times. He was always represented as almost a giant, fording a stream with the infant Jesus on his shoulder, while a hermit on the bank holds a lantern. Invariably the painting of St Christopher faces the principal door of the church. Such a wall painting may be seen at the little church of Baunton, near Cirencester.

This fourteenth century treasure was discovered when plaster was removed a little over 100 years ago and the colours are remarkably fresh and vigorous, whilst the detail is an outstanding example of medieval art.

Another rarity is the fifteenth century embroidered altar frontal. This was also 'discovered' after being used as a tablecloth in a nearby cottage.

NORTH CERNEY

There are many beautiful churches in Britain where love and care have been lavished to restore them to something of their former glory. North Cerney is one of these, and there cannot be any equal to the fascinating stories concerning the collection of the lovely pieces which adorn it. To read the detail is reminiscent of a *Duveen* story, in the world of antiques. Over a period of many years the search was kept up in this country and on the continent for the *right* pieces. From Oxford, Cheltenham, France, Switzerland, Italy, works of art have been collected to adorn this little Cotswold church.

It is certainly one of the most beautifully furnished and colourful in the Cotswolds. Affection has been lavished on it by many people and the mainspring was the Rev. E. W. M. O. de la Hey, who was rector from 1908 until his death in 1936. Much credit is due also to the members of the Croome family, who have been intimately connected with the church for four generations.

This picturesque little church with its saddleback tower, lies just off the main Cheltenham/Cirencester road and was of Saxon foundation. The tower, south door and chancel arch are Norman, the other features mainly Perpendicular. The most rare feature is an incised manticore, which covers several large stones on the outside of the south wall. The reason for its appearance on a church is unknown but mention was made of such a beast in 1529, when it was described as

> *A most strange sort of creature which has the body of a lion, red hair, a face and ears like a man's, three rows of teeth, a sting in their tails like a scorpion's and a very melodious voice.*

As for diet: 'it myght fede on thy Braynes'.

In a slightly different form, the manticore is repeated on the masonry of the belfry turret.

The great restoration of this little church really commenced when the Rev. de la Hey, who was a don at Keble College, Oxford, was appointed to Cerney in 1908. He was a scholar, a man of wide taste, a great collector and, of course, an enthusiast in all he undertook. To restore North Cerney to something of its medieval splendour was a task which he knew would go on beyond his lifetime. He put his knowledge and skill to combing antique shops not only in this country but on the continent as well. Some special pieces he gave to the church and in the purchase of others he was enthusiastically aided by friends.

The actual work began in 1912, when Mr. Croome and his mother decided to completely restore the south transept of the church with its screen as a memorial to Mr. Lancelot Croome, who had been actively interested in the church for many years up to his death. In the course of the work, the medieval high altar was found and its replacement in the chancel naturally led to far greater alterations than at first had been envisaged. To aid the furnishing made necessary by the alterations, the rector was given £100 and this he spent with dealers to very great advantage, purchasing a number of items which included the Persian rug before the high altar, the sixteenth century candlesticks, the chased brass chandelier, wall lights, etc.

While in Brittany, just prior to the 1914 war, the Rev. de la Hey discovered the fine processional cross in a shop at Dinan. One can imagine his excitement as he photographed it, had it checked as genuine by a friend in a London museum and then persuaded friends to make the purchase. This piece was later proved to have come from Poissy, where St. Louis of France was baptised in 1215.

A firm friend of both the Rector and Mr. Croome, was Mr. F. C. Eden, the famous architect, to whom much credit must go for beautifying North Cerney. He designed the reredos as a memorial to two members of the Croome family, the rood loft, screen, the glass in the Lady Chapel and much more. He also persuaded the parishioners to whiten the walls of the church, so making it one of the first to revive the original practise of the medieval church.

The rood loft, which was the gift of Mrs. de la Hey, is an outstanding memorial to the Cerney men who lost their lives in the 1914–18 war.

The story of the figures over the Lady Chapel altar is interesting. Messrs. Eden and Croome found the Madonna standing in the rain on an old chest-of-drawers outside an antique shop in Lugano in 1913. Then for years they searched for a pair to accompany the piece. Sometimes they discovered something they thought would do, but which proved on inspection either too large or too small. Discovery and disappointment went on for years but at last in 1927, this time in Tirano when the Rector was again on holiday, they found two pieces correct to an inch. While the purchase was being made, one of the party foraging in the dark interior of the shop sent a box crashing to the floor and out spilled a fine but dismantled crucifix. It was magnificently carved and was ideal for the rood but Mr. Croome felt they had spent enough. Pressed by his companions he asked the price and the dealer replied: "What, that old

Christ? Oh! £4", at which price the rector acquired it. Today, that piece is a joy to all who see it on the rood in North Cerney's church. It is sixteenth century Italian work.

So the story continued – this labour of love, the ever-present urge to discover the beautiful for the church they loved. The magnificent twenty-light chandelier came from a metal dealer at Cheltenham; a chest from a village cottage; a missal desk from a tallow-chandler's yard in Brescia; a sixteenth century lectern from a marine stores near Gloucester docks; the elaborately carved fifteenth century pulpit; the fifteenth century stained glass windows, and many other items. Through the years the church has been re-furnished to something approaching its medieval appearance before religious intolerance swept away so much that was lovely in all our churches.

North Cerney is a joy both outside and inside and is a 'must' for all who are in the vicinity.

THE "MANTICORE" AS IT APPEARS ON THE SOUTH WALL OF NORTH CERNEY CHURCH

RENDCOMBE

For a very small village Rendcombe has seen more changes than most. In its earliest days it was the seat of the de Clares, Earls of Gloucester, and passing through a succession of great families, was eventually granted by the Crown to Sir Edmund Tame, son of the prosperous wool merchant, who did so much for Fairford church.

In 1840, Sir Francis Goldsmid inherited a substantial fortune on the condition, so the story goes, that he would spend a specified large sum on a country seat. His choice was Rendcomb and the old house was pulled down and the present one erected with Bath stone in the Italian style. The tower was said to have been a copy of that at Osborne House on the Isle of Wight. The stable block was very extensive and is still in being today, although put to other uses. For some reason the spelling of the name of the house differs from the village which has an 'e' on the end of it.

Sir Francis was born in London, the son of Asher Goldsmid, a bullion broker, whose father came to England from Amsterdam. The *Cheltenham Examiner* of the period described him as 'the posessor of enormous wealth'. He was a prominent leader in the Jewish community in England, the first Jewish barrister in Britain, the first Jewish Q.C. and was much respected in Parliament. He was killed in an accident at Waterloo Station in 1878.

The mansion today is occupied by Rendcomb College.

When Edmund Tame went to live at Rendcomb, he emulated his father's good works and early in the sixteenth century built a church. It is thought to show some similarities with the work of the craftsmen who built Fairford church. There is much of interest, particularly the splendid late Norman font, which is a replica of that in Hereford cathedral. The bowl is divided into twelve arched compartments, in which are figured the Apostles – eleven of them – for the space which is occupied by Judas is left "faceless".

Past the stables and through a gate, a pleasant road skirts the woods and winds over the meadows to the village of Chedworth.

A ROMAN VILLA BY THE RIVER COLN

One of the first areas to be subdued and become a Roman province in the year A.D. 43, when the Romans made a serious attempt to conquer Britain, was Gloucestershire. The Roman legions were invincible. They dominated territory across the world with their outposts in Arabia and Britain. In these islands they quickly conquered and settled, and among wealthy Britons the Roman way of life soon became firmly established.

As builders and organisers they had no equals and as the land became pacified their way of life in town and country quickly spread. One of these villas, the country house and farm of a wealthy British family, was built near Chedworth in the valley of the Coln and thanks to the generosity of the former owner, and the patient work of excavators, much of it is still there for us to see. The remains are so well laid out and preserved that the visitor will be a dullard indeed if the imagination is not stirred as he looks upon these striking ruins, which demonstrate so clearly the gracious living of 2,000 years ago.

These remains came to light nearly a hundred years ago, when a game-keeper digging to extricate a ferret, found many fragments of mosaic. The Earl of Eldon was the owner of the land, and when the discovery was brought to his attention, he caused excavations to be made. The results were astounding.

Here set in the very beautiful countryside, this country house in Roman manner has come to life giving a clear-cut impression of the habitation as it was all those centuries ago.

The house was built on the usual plan, three sides of a square. We can see how very clever were the builders of long ago and it gives us a jolt to realise that their device for heating their homes has only in fairly recent years been re-adopted in principle by present-day architects and builders.

The rooms are set out very much as they were. In the dining-room we can see the cavity walls with hollow flue tiles, which enabled the warm air heated by an external furnace, to circulate. The wonder of this room is the mosaic floor, which after being buried for hundreds of years has come to life in its glorious colouring, a beautiful carpet in stone. It is one of the best examples to be found in the west country and is certainly a perfect example of decorative art.

The visitor is left with the impression that the Romans must have been the cleanest people on earth, for there is a whole series of rooms devoted to baths. The bath habit was a serious part of Roman life and so well has the reconstruction of the villa been accomplished, that one can progress through a number of rooms, which in the days of their use were so arranged that the temperature progressively increased. One section was for dry heat, another for damp heat. The water supply came from a spring in the grounds which fed into a 1,500 gallon tank.

There are many living rooms, a steward's room, even latrines, and one can only wonder at the skill and patience of the excavators.

One can feel sorry for the Romanised Britons, whose family may have owned this lovely corner of Gloucestershire for nearly 400 years and then, about the year 409, lost the protection of the empire. The mighty Roman empire was being attacked by the Barbarians and was in difficulties. Outlying Britain was being attacked by the Saxons from the sea, by the tribes from Ireland and by the Picts of Scotland, but things were bad at the heart, and every Roman soldier was required for service at home,

THE INTERIOR OF NORTH CERNEY CHURCH SHOWING THE ROOD

NORTH CERNEY CHURCH

SOME OF THE NINETY-NINE YEWS IN PAINSWICK CHURCHYARD

ONE OF THE LOVELY COTSWOLD VILLAGES — LOWER SLAUGHTER

THE OLD TITHE BARN AT SYDE. THE LOWER PART WAS THOUGHT TO HAVE BEEN THE PRIEST'S DWELLING

ONE OF THE BEAUTIFUL ECCLESIASTICAL WINDOWS IN THE PRIEST'S DWELLING AT SYDE

A PRETTY CORNER
AT STANTON

THE MOSAIC FLOOR AT CHEDWORTH IS A GLORY OF COLOUR

SIX OF THE SEVEN SPRINGS OF BISLEY

A TYPICAL COTSWOLD SCENE

FEW OF THE FINE COTSWOLD SHEEP REMAIN. THIS ONE IS OF THE LAST FLOCK ON THE HILLS AT ALDSWORTH

THE WONDERFUL HONEY COLOURED WALLS, BUILT TO ENDURE BY MASTER CRAFTSMEN

HOUNDS OF THE HEYTHROP HUNT AT LOWER SLAUGHTER

THE LOFTY CHANCEL ARCH OF BIBURY CHURCH WITH SAXON MASONRY IN THE JAMBS

SNOWSHILL MANOR. THE STEPS THAT LEAD TO THE ORNAMENTAL GARDENS.

A SPRING MORNING ON THE FOSSE WAY NEAR CIRENCESTER.

THE LOVELY NORMAN CHANCEL AT ELKSTONE IN WHICH THERE IS ALWAYS A GOLDEN GLOW. NOTE THE DRAGONS' HEADS—AN UNUSUAL FEATURE WHICH TERMINATES THE PELLETED HOOD MOULD

THE UNUSUAL CHIMNEY AT BLISS MILLS, CHIPPING NORTON

THE MANOR HOUSE NEXT TO THE CHURCH AT UPPER SWELL

A COTSWOLD STUDY IN BLACK AND WHITE

ONE OF THE FOUR SAXON CARVINGS IN DAGLINGWORTH CHURCH. THIS ONE DEPICTS THE CRUCIFIXION

THE UNIQUE MONUMENT IN BISLEY CHURCHYARD WHICH KEEPS ALIVE THE STORY OF THE "BISLEY PIECE" IN BIBURY CHURCHYARD

THE ROAD TO PAINSWICK

THE HEART MEMORIAL IN COBERLEY CHURCH

COBERLEY CHURCH IN ITS LOVELY SETTING

so the Roman Legions had to return. The Britons were told to defend themselves, and with the collapse of the province came the break-up of civilised life. Much that was good perished, including this delightful villa in a superb corner of the English countryside, where the spring which fed the baths so long ago still trickles on its way.

In 1924, Chedworth was purchased and presented to the National Trust. It is easily approached by two main roads, the Cheltenham/Northleach Road (A.40) or the Northleach/ Cirencester Road (A.429). The fact that the villa is named 'Chedworth' is confusing, for it is some four miles' distance from that village, but just a mile from Yanworth village.

It is open daily, including Sundays and Bank Holidays (but not on other Mondays or during the first week of November) until 7 p.m. or dusk, if earlier.

NORTHLEACH

In the great days of the wool trade there were three principal centres at which the merchants congregated – Burford, Cirencester and Northleach. Of these the latter took pride of place. One ancient chronicler records that in the fifteenth century, at the annual showing of wool samples, almost every European language could be heard in the streets of Northleach. It must have been a very busy, besides prosperous town, but today it has little to show for its past splendour, except the magnificent church which ranks with the best of the Shire.

Much love and wealth was lavished on it by the wool merchants and one in particular, John Fortey, who rebuilt the nave, was very generous. The porch of the church is two storied and it is considered the most beautiful in England. Its upper windows are surrounded by rich arcading and between them is a panel containing images of the Holy Trinity and the

Virgin set in niches. The upper room of the porch has a fireplace, with a cunningly arranged smoke vent or chimney between the bracketed pinnacles. An effective reminder that in days gone by there was a priest living there.

Inside, the church is full of interest. There is a triple sedilia, a sign, perhaps, of the ancient splendour of the church. A memorial brass to John Fortey, the chief benefactor, who died in 1548, shows him in the simple garb of a merchant with one foot resting on a sheep, the other on a woolpack. Apparently churches were not his only interest, for he is described as a renovator of roads *and* churches. The fascinating pictorial stops between each word of the eulogy on the memorial should be noted. A crab, a hedgehog, a cock, oak leaves, etc., are probably unique in this form.

An older brass depicts another merchant standing on a woolpack and at his wife's feet is a tiny dog, which is looking up at its mistress and displaying with pride, it seems, the bells on the collar round his neck.

There is a well-known mensa at Northleach, which is ten feet in length and weighs nearly a ton. The mensa was the high altar in the medieval church and it was decreed that it must be of stone and in one piece. It was supported by two pillars of masonry and stood about 3 ft high. Five incised crosses marked on it represented the five wounds of Christ. In the thirteenth century the altar slab had to take this form, but in 1550, the Bishops ordered the removal of all stone altars. Not only were they removed but the greater majority were broken up or used as paving stones or even, as at Wyck Rissington, used as a tombstone.

THE STORY OF THE WOOL TRADE

Much of England's history and wealth was built on the wool trade and there is no doubt that in the middle ages, the fine wool from this country put England in a premier position. The wool was exported to the great cloth-making centres of the continent, where it was turned into cloth of excellent quality and sent all over the world.

The reason for England's virtual monopoly in wool was twofold. The low lying lands of northern Europe were excellent for running great flocks of sheep but the country was the 'cock-pit' of Europe and was continually being fought over, a horror which England escaped. Secondly, the wolf was exterminated in this country after the Conquest but flourished in the continental forests until the sixteenth century. Between the warfare of men and the marauding of wolves, it was impossible to keep sheep on any scale, so the foreigners had to come to England for wool.

From the twelfth to the fifteenth century in particular, England's commerce and her politics were built upon the commodity. It financed the wars over a long period, provided the ransom for King Richard I and above all, it proved an easy method of raising taxes for a variety of other purposes, which monarchs thought up from time to time.

In 1297, it was recorded that the wool of England amounted to half the value of the whole land, for wool entered into every phase of English life. Not only agricultural workers and the middle classes, but the wealthy classes and the monasteries depended in no small degree upon the humble sheep for their livelihood.

The shepherd was an important man and enjoyed many special rights and privileges:

> *'He enjoyed a bowl of whey all through the summer and the milk of ewes on a Sunday. A lamb at weaning time and a fleece at shearing.'*

The great abbeys such as Tintern and Abbey Dore, derived much of their great wealth from wool. In 1350, the Abbot of

Cirencester, who at that time possessed the sole rights to weigh wool, had accommodation in his warehouses for some 20,000 bales. One community of nuns grazed nearly 2,000 ewes on Minchinhampton Common.

By the fifteenth century, Cotswold sheep were producing the very finest quality wool, surpassed only by Shropshire and Herefordshire breeds.

In the fourteenth century the best wool was priced at 28 marks per sack of 254-lb, and a mark was worth 13s. 4d. The annual export value was some seven million pounds.

Thus the wool merchants of the Cotswolds became immeasurably wealthy. Well might the merchant of a Cotswold town engrave on the windows of his fine new house:—

"*I praise God and ever shall*
It is the sheep hath paid for it all".

There are still examples of the houses the wool merchants built in Northleach.

In the seventeenth century, however, the wool trade declined and in spite of every effort made to resuscitate it, never regained its fifteenth century eminence. One attempt to stimulate the industry was made in 1667, when an Act of Parliament made it punishable for 'a corps of any person to be buried in any stuffe or thing other than what is made of sheep's wool only'. It was a belated effort to halt the decline in trade by reducing imports of linen from abroad. To make for a more vigorous observance of the Act, an amendment was made in 1678, requiring a properly attested certificate to be produced before any funeral took place, with a fine of five pounds for non-compliance. The money was divided between the informer and the poor. Although the Act was never popular, it was not repealed until 1800, but it fell into disuse long before.

Very few of the original Cotswold breed of sheep remain today, in fact the only flock of any size is at Aldworthy, near

Bibury. The large size of the breed is the chief reason for its decline. Today the housewife requires a small joint and a minimum of fat. The day when a 5-lb joint of Cotswold mutton was the basis of the Sunday meal, has long passed.

The quality of the wool is coarse and, therefore, among the lowest priced per pound. Moreover, the average lamb per ewe is only just over one per year, which is a low average compared with many other breeds. By way of compensation, the size of the fleece of a Cotswold sheep is larger than any other, with the possible exception of the Lincoln, and the staple is quite 6 in. in length. Needless to say, the better fed they are the heavier the fleece, but here again as the breed is essentially a root eating sheep, the question of economics comes in.

However, the Cotswold hills are still great sheep country and at a conservative estimate, there are not less than 50,000 ewes still grazing in the area.

COTSWOLD STONE

A large part of the charm of the Cotswold villages is of course due to the stone, which when weathered takes on a lovely golden-honey-coloured hue, but the finer points of the craftsmanship which went into the work of the cottages and buildings in the past is fast being omitted, due to the lack of craftsmen.

Fifty or sixty years ago there were a great many quarries working, which produced large quantities of stone for building, for slating and dry-walling, and a considerable number of specialist craftsmen were employed. There was the banker mason who shaped the stone in the quarry, the master mason, the quarryman, the slater and the dry stone-waller.

The type of stone varied considerably from quarry to quarry. That used for building had a tighter grain than was used for other purposes. It was cut out in large blocks of some

$2\frac{1}{2}$ feet square and sawn to shape as required, with a large steel cross-cut saw.

Coscombe quarry, near Guiting Power, was known for this tight grain of stone (similar to Bath stone), which made it ideal for building and on one occasion a single block weighing eight tons was sent away. It proved too big to handle at its destination and such a size was never repeated. There used to be specially constructed stone carrying waggons, drawn by four stalwart horses to take the stone to the rail head.

The work was hard and the hours long. Mr. Robert Worvell, of Guiting Power, who had a retentive memory when over eighty years of age, worked Cotswold stone for most of his active life. A nine-hour day and a sixty-hour week on piece-work was real toil. When the stone was dug out it was measured and the men were paid accordingly. They earned perhaps thirty shillings per week. There are, of course, many quarries still working but these special craftsmen are fast disappearing.

For the last twenty-one years of his life until retirement at sixty-six years of age, Mr. Worvell cycled the seven miles from Guiting Power to Farmington quarry and back every day in all weathers. In the village of Cold Aston, through which he used to pass, they set their clocks by him.

The making of the Cotswold roofing slates was a thriving industry, for every building – cottage, house, barn or church – had its Cotswold slate roof. To obtain it, ground in the quarry was cleared to a depth of some 2 ft and the stone was removed in blocks and laid on the surface to wait for nature with its frosts, to do the work of splitting it. Frost would cause the seams to lift and spread. Craftsmen then shaped the tiles and with a special small pick would with a deft tap, make a hole in it for fixing. It was rare that there was enough stone accumulated for all the year round work, though there were often whole fields laid out with it. The work, therefore, became seasonal and naturally when other full-time employment became available the men took it. At the peak period, Huntsman's quarry, near Guiting, which specialised in the slating, employed nearly a hundred men. It is still working, supplying crazy paving, hard core and walling stone.

Farmington quarry, near Northleach, has been worked for about 200 years and the stone is used mostly for building. From the quarry, material has recently been supplied for a new wing of St. Anne's College, Oxford, and a bank in a Cotswolds town, London's Temple church was also rebuilt with the stone after the war.

The section of the quarry being worked today is some 50 ft deep, and it is interesting to watch a stone weighing 75 lb being cleared and split with the aid of an iron bar. The stone once excavated, is taken to the top by crane and then a hole is made in each side of the block. Known as 'dog holes' they give purchase to the hook of the lifting tackle. They then 'clear one bed', which means chip off the ragged layer, leaving a fairly smooth surface. It is an education to watch the men clean this surface by swinging a double-headed axe and paring off as little, if need be, as an eighth of an inch. The stone, cleaned up, is then taken to the cutting shed where it is placed on a wheeled platform and then whilst water is poured on to it, cut to the required dimensions with a large circular carborundum saw. The texture of the stone varies and sometimes even a six inch length will take over an hour to cut. A specially hard stone has a grain and a glaze like marble. As the foreman remarked, "anything five million years old like this ought to be hard". Much of the stone is cut for fireplaces and often has to be correct to an eighth-of-an-inch. Lengths up to 7 ft can be cut by the carborundum saws and the men who work them are mason-sawyers and, of course real experts.

In another part of the yard the banker masons are at work, shaping the stone to special requirements. Ornamental balls for gate pillars, finials, pinnacles and gables or cornice pieces. To shape a ball they have no special tools or measuring instruments other than a blacksmith's rasp and a drag. Most reliance is placed on the sure eye and touch of the craftsman.

The small stone is little used today as there are not the men available to shape it, even for dry walling, so it remains at the foot of the quarry, perhaps eventually to come to light in another five million years.

HAMPNETT

Half-a-mile from Northleach and just off the Northleach/Stow road is the hamlet of Hampnett. The church is ancient but was restored in 1868 at a cost of £700. It was £700 wasted! Originally there was a central tower, but it was demolished and like Elkstone it now has a two compartment chancel. The lovely symmetry of the Norman work is ruined by thc unhappy reproductions and imitations of early wall paintings, but the churchwardens are hoping to remove some of them when funds permit.

Hampnett must have had something that proved irresistible to courting couples in days gone by, for the tiny place saw the celebration of no less than 346 marriages in the seventeen years between 1737 and 1754. Not all of them were local weddings, some of the couples came from neighbouring counties, which would account for the belief that it was a lucky church in which to be married.

The monster barn opposite the church is really magnificent, as indeed are many of the other farm buildings and some of the houses.

The road from Hampnett continues towards Turkdean and passes through a superb avenue of beech trees, which are are at their best in the autumn.

TURKDEAN

Turkdean church was built as a penance by a Norman knight to make up for a life of cruelty and greed. It has much of interest for the visitor and its position with the manor farm (which incidentally contains part of a twelfth century crypt) and the manor house adjoining, make an attractive group.

NOTGROVE

The road continues to Notgrove and yet another group of buildings, which show how the church in days gone by was the centre of the community. Here are the manor farm, Glebe House, the manor house, all within a stone's throw of each other. This was the village where the Whittington family resided in the fifteenth and sixteenth centuries. Three of them have tombs in the church – Alexander, who was a knight, Christopher and one of their sisters.

The font is a fine specimen, lead-lined with bands of cable moulding beneath the rim, and is one of the best shaped in the county.

There are only five churches in Gloucestershire without an east window. Notgrove is one with this unusual feature.

On the east wall of the church is a vast modern tapestry, which illustrates in its design the church and village. This remarkable piece was worked by Lady Anderson and her family, at the adjoining Manor.

BIBURY

Bibury is a village of great beauty situated on the banks of the river Coln. There is a fine old mill at one end and the world-famous cottage group – Arlington Row – at the other. The cottages, grey walled, grey roofed and gabled, are considered a perfect example of how cottages ought to look. Picturesque they certainly are.

Running through the gardens of the Swan hotel is one of the finest streams in the Cotswolds. It comes from the great oolite limestone and is remarkably cold. It is believed that this was the reason the road bridge was built in 1779, for cattle hot through travel, were chilled as they forded the stream.

Up to the middle of the eighteenth century, the district was famous for the Bibury Club and old ordnance maps mark the racecourse between Bibury and Burford. It was complete even to its grandstand and was a very popular meeting – patronised by the Prince Regent himself. It ended with the Enclosure Act of 1775.

The church, in the centre of a cluster of cottages and houses, is a joy, and the churchyard, is a model of how such grounds should be maintained. Clean and tidy with the paths bordered by standard roses, it gives a feeling of peace and care – in marked contrast to many churchyards with their uncut grass, a tangle of growth and tombs leaning this way and that as if part of a drunken orgy.

There was a stone-built church at Bibury before the Normans came and lengthened the nave and added the aisles. The tower is Early English (about 1230). The windows of the Decorated period on the north aisle are very lovely and an unusual feature is a Saxon sepulchural stone enriched with interlacing circles. The lofty but narrow chancel arch contains Saxon masonry in the jambs. Altogether this is an inspiring church.

As mentioned under Bisley village, there is a part of the churchyard here known as the 'Bisley piece'. Some of the older folk in Bibury remember their forebears speaking of a cross-country path to Bisley being known as Dead Man's Lane, and it actually appears as such on old maps.

Close by is Bibury Court, built in 1623.

The river and surrounding streams which meander pleasantly around Bibury, abound with fish. They can be seen swimming in the river, or perhaps on a summer's evening rising for flies. The stream on the south side of the village which runs round Arlington Row, contains in its banks quite a colony of water vole. Fascinating little fellows and quick as lightning, one has to be quiet to see them and having done so, hope that the cats at the nearby hatchery stay put!

A further asset to the natural beauty of the village is a number of ornamental duck, Canada geese and mallard, the antics of which are also a source of interest.

THE TROUT FARM

Near the seventeenth century picturesque old cloth mill is the famous trout hatchery which has been in existence since 1900. Prior to 1948, the hatchery was worked and cared for by the famous fisherman and naturalist, the late Arthur Severn. A devoted countryman, he played a very active part in the church and village life of Bibury.

The hatchery is now run on commercial lines. There are five acres of ponds and the fish are graded according to size, to reduce to a minimum the cannibalistic tendencies of the fish. At a peak period the ponds may contain hundreds of thousands of fish for which there is a very heavy demand all over the country. Both rainbow and brown trout are bred and sold in varying degrees of size from the ova upwards.

The characteristics of the two fish are very different. The brown variety can, in the wild state, attain a weight of up to nine pounds, but in the hatchery, three pounds is an average. They will rarely move two or three hundred yards from where they are bred or put into the river except perhaps in the mating season, but they generally return. The rainbow is a much more temperamental fish, faster growing and attaining a weight of five or six pounds. This fish is inclined to wander and, therefore, does better in lakes or ponds.

With such a large number of fish, feeding can be quite a problem and their diet is fifty per cent. offal, to give a fresh carnivorous diet and fifty per cent. pellets, made up to a special formula and including barley meal, oil, etc.

Recently ova, frozen in ice, has been sent to various parts of the world by air with great success. The grown fish are transported in special tanks and fed with oxygen, so that they arrive at their destination as fresh as they left the breeding pools.

Like every other undertaking this business has its hazards. The heron accounts for a very large number of fish. The kingfisher and water shrew take their share of the smaller ones. The water voles play havoc by their activities damaging the sides of the ponds. The several cats on the 'staff' of the hatchery do, however, keep this to a minimum.

The trout farm is open to the public on certain days in the spring and summer.

CHALFORD – The Alpine Village

Chalford's history goes back to the fourteenth century, and enjoyed a new lease of life in the seventeenth century when many of its residents were wealthy clothiers.

In the Golden valley some three miles from Stroud, Chalford is typical of many of the Cotswold villages, which due to their inaccessibility have not altered very much since those early days. Said to be the second largest village in England, its twisting streets are terraced in the steep hillside, indeed some of the houses and cottages seem quite precariously perched. Many cottages give the impression that long ago their owners staked a claim on the hillside and soon finding it too small, began to burrow into the hillside to make room for a kitchen or an extra room. This in fact is what has happened over the years. The main street, the only real street in Chalford, twists and turns higher and higher up the hillside, until from the top an enchanting view of this unique place is obtainable. Until the 1920's the bread for the whole village was delivered by *Jennie*, the donkey. With two large pannier baskets across her back, she did the job for the best part of thirty years.

Another chapter in Chalford's industrial history opened in 1779, when the Stroudwater & Wallbridge canal, which had been discussed for fifty years, eventually materialised. It was closed in 1933, but there are still many interesting remains to be seen.

The ingenuity of man in the earlier days of sheer necessity, has used the Cotswold stone in a hundred ways. Walls, gullies, troughs, roof slates and even flower pots in Chalford are of the local stone.

Here the city planners have met their Waterloo. Under no conceivable circumstances can they widen the road to take a coach, or re-plan, or build 'flyovers', for there is not room to place as much as an extra dustbin, and a good thing too. Chalford is quite fascinating just as it is.

THE COMMONS & VILLAGES NEAR STROUD

The lovely commons, Minchinhampton and Rodborough, south of the Golden valley, are both National Trust properties. Minchinhampton village was once a cloth-making centre and the picturesque pillared town hall, built in 1698, is a vivid reminder of that era. Nearby are two interesting items. Tom Long's Post, a signpost where six roads meet, marks the burial place of a highwayman who committed suicide, rather than be captured. On an unclassified road leading to the village of Avening, is the *Long Stone*, part of an ancient Barrow. Babies used to be passed through the hole in its centre, to ensure a complete cure for rickets. Rodborough Fort, the castellated mansion which crowns the common, is a familiar landmark. It is an excellent point for extensive views but has no history.

AVENING village is famous for its annual Pig's Face Feast. The church is a fine one and contains in the north transcept a monument to Henry Brydges, a son of Lord Chandos. Henry was a wild character indeed, but eventually he settled down and married the heiress of the eminent clothier, Samuel Sheppard, who was the local lord of the manor. The monument shows the once wild freebooter kneeling in prayer.

At AMBERLEY, also near Minchinhampton common, Mrs. Dinah Maria Craik wrote her novel *John Halifax, Gentleman*, which was published in 1857 and achieved great popularity with Victorians. The novel was set in Tewkesbury. Rose Cottage, where the authoress lived, is still to be seen.

In this area many of the wealthy clothmakers had their houses, although there had always been wealthy families as lords of the manors. The fine house, Lypiatt and its park, which occupies a commanding position on a plateau overlooking Stancombe, near Bisley, has had an interesting history. During the Civil war it was garrisoned by the troops of Parliament, but was captured by Sir Jacob Astley, who marched over from Cirencester for the purpose.

John Stephens, the owner of the house at that time, was sympathetic to the Parliamentary cause but he was also related to both Cromwell and Ireton.

Near Miserden is the residence once known as Eagle house, by reason of the great stone eagles (really griffins) which decorate the top of the facade. When war broke out in 1914, the owner felt that as the eagle was the emblem of the German empire, it was expedient to change it, so the house became as it is today, Hazel Manor. The property once belonged to Henry VIII.

There is a story that one who took an active part in the trial of Bishop Hooper, subsequently burned at the stake in Gloucester in 1555, lived in this house. Afterwards, filled with remorse, he hanged himself in a corridor at the top of the house, where a giant nail used in the macabre proceedings is still in place.

THE SEVEN SPRINGS OF BISLEY

The road from Chalford leads to Bisley another village with a long history.

From time immemorial there have been seven springs gushing from the hillside into a lane in the village, and only within living memory have they been directed into spouts and troughs. The story goes that they supplied baths for the monks long ago. Of course, the older generation drank the water all their lives, but some twenty or so years ago it was condemned for drinking purposes. Some of the more cynical villagers say that the condemnation came at a time when the authorities were bringing main water to the village and were meeting with opposition. Like all traditional streams and wells, these seven springs were accorded special healing properties.

Every Ascension day after a special service in the church, a procession of children proceeds to the streams. The spouts are decorated with flowers and the ceremony is sufficiently picturesque to have been twice the subject of television broadcasts.

In the churchyard is a unique monument some 600 to 700 years old. Six-sided with stone seats, it has a miniature spire and delicate shafts. It covers a vault or 'bone hole', which is said to be full of bones from the graveyard. But there is an interesting story told that it covers a former well, into which one dark night the parish priest tumbled and was drowned. In due course, news of the unfortunate happening reached the Pope, who not only ordered the erection of a monument but as a punishment to the parishioners for their negligence, cancelled the right of burial at Bisley for a period of two years. To make things even more difficult, he decreed that parishioners should be buried at Bibury, fifteen miles across country. Fact or fiction? The fact does remain that to this day a portion of Bibury's churchyard is known as 'the Bisley piece'. (See page 90).

The church suffered considerable rebuilding in the middle of the nineteenth century, but still has many items of great interest. Two wooden figures, which formerly were part of the roof decoration, are now lodged on a window sill. Very ancient, they represent a man playing bagpipes and another, a recorder.

MISERDEN

Miserden is three miles from Bisley. Its church is of Saxon origin but after restoration again in thc nineteenth century, little was left undisturbed except the tower and fortunately the monuments in the manor chapel in the south aisle.

The absorbing thing about monumental sculpture is that we can see how our ancestors looked, how they dressed, how they were armed and often, which were their favourite pets. All these things are immediately apparent in the magnificent tomb of Sir William Sandys and his lady, Margaret, in Miserden church. Sir William is in full armour, so detailed that the hinges of the leg armour look real. His face and beard are finely chiselled and the lady's gown with its lacework is in graceful folds. At the lady's feet is a very vicious falcon looking spiteful, yet elegant. At the knight's feet is a griffin attacking another falcon. The carving is superb and the alabaster figures look alive. Round the sides of the tomb are effigies of the Sandys' children. Of the three young men in the dress of cavaliers, two hold skulls before them, to denote that they died before their parents. There are three elder daughters, one of which also holds a skull, and at one end of the tomb are three very small children in clothes to show they died before baptism. Above the tomb are the helm, sword and gauntlets of the knight.

So beautiful is this memorial – undoubtedly one of the best in the country – that it was thought by some authorities to be the work of the great sculptor, Nicholas Stone, who was master mason to Charles I. The present descendants of the Sandys, however, have documentary proof that portraits were sent to Italy *before* their deaths and the effigies were modelled from them. The alabaster is Italian, and the cost of the monument was £1,000. The date effectively settled the controversy, as to whether the memorial was the work of Stone, though it is a compliment to whoever was responsible for its execution.

Close by is the effigy of another Tudor knight in armour. At his feet is a goat nibbling a cabbage. He was the son of Sir William Kingston, who was buried in Painswick church.

A fine west window, given by the Nizam of Hyderabad in memory of the rector's twenty-eight-year-old son who had served the Nizam is unfortunately completely covered by a massive organ pipe.

Pat Smythe, the world-famous horsewoman, lives in the village, where she breeds horses. It was here that she trained the horses which became household names in the early sixties. Flanagan, Scorchin, Tosca, Prince Hal, and others. She was Britain's leading woman show jumper from the time she first represented Britain in 1947. In the 1956 Olympics at Stockholm, she won a bronze medal and was three times woman champion of Europe. Miss Smythe married a Swiss businessman and is now Mrs. Koechlin.

A COTSWOLD GAME FARM

High up, in the country between Miserden and Stroud, is the Cotswold Game farm, which from very small beginnings in 1923, has grown until it is today a fascinating and thriving industry.

The idea of supplying game birds first occurred to Mr. P. R. Symonds over forty-five years ago, when before the days of incubators it was usual for game-keepers from estates in the Gloucestershire area to travel the countryside searching for broody hens which could be used to hatch out pheasant and partridge eggs.

Mr. Symonds quickly saw that there was need for a service of this nature and so he established an organisation to meet it, and by 1939, with the rearing of some 27,000 pheasants per year the farm was a success. Many types of game birds were stocked. In addition to the English pheasant and partridge, Hungarian partridges were imported from Czechoslovakia and other places, and in reverse a thriving export market was built up. The coming of the war, however, all but closed the farm except for a very small nucleus and now a tremendous increase in production, supplies not only much of the home market but Europe as well, when 70 per cent of eggs or chicks are exported. Pheasant, partridge, mallard, golden silver and the American Bob White quail are now bred.

The birds are penned up for laying in March and the farm either sells the eggs; hatches them and supplies day old chicks or rears them up to six, eight or twelve weeks old. The figures are quite amazing. Four thousand, five hundred birds are penned for laying and not more than six to a pen. Altogether some fifteen thousand eggs, which require twenty-four days to hatch out, are set each week for a sixteen week period.

In this twentieth century, one is accustomed to science creeping in on most things, but it is surprising to the layman that the modern incubators used on the farm have been made to achieve almost a broody hen instinct. As a hen when she is sitting turns the eggs over gradually, so does the modern machine by gradually tilting the trays containing the eggs, achieve exactly the same result. The correct amount of air and humidity is automatically supplied and a fan is switched on and off as needed. During the three weeks the eggs are in the incubator, one hundred degrees of heat is constant.

It has been found, however, that no single type of incubator can satisfactorily hatch a game egg, so that when the eggs have been in the first machine for twenty days, they are transferred to another type of equipment which provides still air. After the incubation period, the eggs are tested under a strong artificial light and the number which prove non-fertile amount to a very small percentage indeed. When the eggs are hatched, it is quite fascinating to watch the thousands of tiny chicks showing such life and immediate energy.

These chicks travel extremely well, they can manage quite comfortably for twenty-four hours without food and in pre-war days, enormous numbers used to be sent to Belgium by rail and sea without trouble. Air travel makes transport much easier today, though the formalities of export customs etc., take far longer than the time it used to take a whole consignment of birds to accomplish a long journey. Modern balanced foods for the birds in their early months have made a tremendous improvement in the stock, and the season for breeding has in recent years consequently been much extended.

PAINSWICK

Painswick is one of the famous villages of Gloucestershire, perhaps more than anything else for the story of the ninety-nine yews in the churchyard. It is said that despite all efforts to grow one hundred, one will always wither and die. The devil, they say, comes in the night and takes its life. The village is certainly very beautifully situated and has some architectural gems among its buildings – the Court House near the church with its tall chimneys and graceful line, Beacon House, the Vicarage and many more.

Painswick Beacon is beautiful in any season, but with its autumn colouring surpasses description.

History has not passed this attractive village by, for it was the scene of at least two skirmishes during the Civil Wars. In 1644, Cromwell's troops took up a defensive position in the churchyard and when pressed retreated into the church itself. Thereupon the cavaliers set fire to the doors and cast in 'hand-grenadoes'. The marks of these and other shot on the north side of the tower, and traces of the fire are still evident.

A Royal proclamation exists which, issued by the King, and headed 'Given at our Court at Payneswick 1643' forbade soldiers to rob or molest the country people when they brought their provisions in for sale to the market installed there.

In the sixteenth century, the Lord of the manor of Painswick was Sir William Kingston, who was quite an important personage and must have been what we would today describe as a 'tough guy'. He fought at the Battle of Flodden in 1513, and then became Constable of the Tower of London. In that capacity he had to arrest Cardinal Wolsey and later, Anne Boleyn. He presided over that poor lady's execution. Kingston was taken in a fit in Painswick and died in 1540. His family must have decided that he should rest as he had lived, and appear to have stolen a very handsome canopy tomb of Purbeck marble in the church, in which someone had lain for two hundred years. Nearly a hundred years later, the platform of the tomb was used for kneeling effigies of yet others, so honours are even.

The church dates back to the twelfth century but it was largely re-built two hundred years later. The western tower was surmounted by a fine spire which was struck by lightning in 1883, and crashed to the ground. At a cost of £1,500 it was re-built by the parishioners and remains a fine landmark, as indeed it must have except for a short interval since 1632.

Outside the churchyard are the village stocks and whipping post. There is said to be only one similar set of these 'Spectacle' stocks in the country. A stone seat for the wrong-doers who occupied them, does not look very comfortable, to say the least of it.

Beyond Painswick on the Cheltenham Road is the *Adam & Eve* inn (which once upon a time was kept by a man named Abel), and the road on the right leads *downhill* to a place aptly named Paradise – surely a new conception of paradise.

The country is especially lovely in this area – Cranham Woods, Sheepscombe – altogether an ideal area for the visitor to see glorious Gloucestershire within a small compass.

in 1643, and razed to the ground. At a cost of £1,500 it was rebuilt by the parishioners and remains a fine landmark, as indeed it must have except for a short interval since 1643.

Outside the churchyard are the village stocks and whipping post. There is said to be only one similar set of these 'Spectacle' stocks in the country. A stone seat for the wrong-doers who occupied them, does not look very comfortable, to say the least of it.

Beyond Painswick on the Cheltenham Road is the *Adam & Eve* inn (which once upon a time was kept by a man named Abel), and the road on the right leads downhill to a place aptly named Paradise—surely a new conception of paradise.

The country is especially lovely in this area – Cranham Woods, Sheepscombe – altogether an ideal area for the visitor to see glorious Gloucestershire within a small compass.

EAST COTSWOLDS

CHIPPING NORTON

The thriving market town of Chipping Norton is in Oxfordshire and is said to be the highest in the country. The streets seem to rise one above the other, as if designed in tiers. The market place is always busy and at one end is the Guildhall. Even for an old Cotswold town, the number of inns which are in or near the market place is remarkable. The *White Hart*, *Blue Boar*, *Chequers* and *King's Arms* are only some of them, each with an attractive sign. All are old and typical of the coaching era.

The church is a fine Perpendicular building, entered through a medieval porch but perhaps the most unique feature is the fact that there are two north aisles. The fifteenth century font is outstanding for the delicate tracery with which it is adorned. There are too, a number of fifteenth century brasses, with interesting portraits including the inevitable wool merchant who stands on two woolpacks.

In the churchyard are a large number of tombstones carved from Cotswold stone. A remarkable tribute on one of them is to the wife of a ratcatcher:—

Here lieth the body of Phillis
wife of John Humphreys
Rat catcher
who was lodged in many a town
and travelled far and near
by age and death she is struck down
to her last lodging here. 1763

Close to the church are the ancient almshouses which were built in 1640 by Henry Cornish, a local man.

An Industrial Romance

When during the religious troubles of the sixteenth century, the Huguenots were driven from the Low Countries, many of them settled in the Cotswold valleys round about Stroud. Some of the exiles were highly skilled in weaving and cloth-making and this, coupled with the fact that the water of the district was ideal for the purpose, soon built up a thriving industry. It was particularly fortunate, as it helped to replace the wool trade which was then in its decline.

The attention of visitors is often attracted to the Bliss mills which are situated in the valley by Chipping Norton. The odd shape of the dome from which rises the chimney of the mill seems somehow incongruous in such a setting.

The mill had its beginnings some 200 years ago, when a Chalford man, Thomas Bliss, started in business on his own account and quickly became known for the very fine quality of the cloth he manufactured. Bliss's father was a cloth manufacturer who operated from Chalford and young Bliss used to carry his samples round the Cotswold towns. It was on one of his trips to Chipping Norton that he fell in love and subsequently married the daughter of the landlord of the *Swan* Inn, who, liking Bliss, purchased for him a small manufactory, specialising in *tiltings* for covering carts, light woollen *linseys* for women's petticoats and *rugging* for horses.

This first business was conducted from, of all places, the Vicarage, the yarn being spun on spinning wheels in the cottages of Chipping Norton and the surrounding villages. With the whole family (there were ten in all) and the women of the district assisting this family concern, trade rapidly increased. First it was moved to a malt house, then a nearby flour mill was added, but this had its drawbacks, as it was dependent upon water for power. There was no water for four months in the year and in a dry season it was longer.

Horse clothing had become a speciality and in fact, it was supplied direct to the royal stables at Buckingham Palace. It is noteworthy that, at that time, everything was being cut by old hand shears which, incidentally, were sent to Nailsworth *once a year* for sharpening.

In 1816, William Bliss (the second generation) retired through ill-health and his fourteen-year-old son, Robert, instead of continuing school took over the management of the business. Eight years later he emigrated to America, leaving an aunt in charge, and one can imagine the surprise in Chipping Norton when six years later, he returned with an American bride.

In 1839, another William Bliss took over the mill and it was he who had the greatest impact on its fortunes. Records show that the weekly wage bill at the commencement of his management was £17, but thirty-eight years later it had risen to £500 a week. The mill was enlarged and turnover increased out of all proportion to its humble beginnings. In 1851, at the Crystal Palace exhibition, the firm was awarded two first-class medals for shawls and tweeds. Success bred success, and at exhibitions in New York and Paris, royal awards were gained by the firm. In 1867, William Bliss – an Englishman – was awarded the French Emperor's prize of £500 for the employer who had done most to promote the welfare of his work-people.

Then in 1872 there was a calamity, when in the space of two hours fire destroyed most of the mill. Undaunted, however, another mill was planned which was to be of the best design, completely fireproof and at the same time architecturally ornamental. Fulfilling all those purposes, it was completed within twelve months and not a stone of the old building was used.

The dome which often arouses curiosity, was planned with a stairway on the inside of it. On the parapet of the dome, some small repairs were carried out many years ago, and in this slap-dash twentieth century, a handful of cement would have done the job. Not so with the Cotswold craftsman who was responsible. A 2 in. cube of stone was carefully cut to shape and set in so well that the joint is only just discernible. This is sixty odd feet above ground and on an outside cornice where, of course, it is only seen at times of inspection. Well may we talk of pride of craftsmanship. The parapet of the dome is 64 ft. from the ground and the chimney itself rises to 165 ft. There was a bell fixed at the dome level to ring the times of working hours, and keenly progressive, the mill was the first in Britain to be run by electricity.

The Bliss Mills still operate, although today no longer owned by the Bliss family, who relinquished control in 1916. Fine cloth still leaves the valley for countries as far afield as U.S.A., Australia, New Zealand, Japan, Hong Kong, South Africa and most European countries.

It is interesting, too, that though the wool trade virtually died in the Cotswolds, its successor, the cloth trade, gave employment and prosperity to towns and villages over a wide area. This too, has sadly declined over the years and today the whole of the west of England produces but a small percentage of the wool cloth made in this country.

The Rollright Stones

Not far from Chipping Norton, are the mysterious Rollright Stones. There are seventy-seven of them, which form a circle 100 ft. in diameter and no one knows either their origin or purpose. Cut from local limestone, they have not weathered well over the years. On the opposite side of the road is the King's Stone, 80 ft. high, which stands in solitary splendour. Four hundred yards away is a smaller group of five stones, known as the Whispering Knights.

SHIPTON-UNDER-WYCHWOOD

This quiet little village on the main road from Burford to Chipping Norton, has much of interest within its boundaries. The fountain on the edge of the village green commemorates the seventeen local men who sailed with hundreds of other immigrants to New Zealand in 1874. The ship caught fire and of the 500 souls on board there were only three survivors. Opposite is the *Shaven Crown*, an inn with a long history. It was originally a pilgrims' hostel connected with Bruern Abbey. Later it became the property of the parish, and when it was sold in 1927, the capital was invested and the interest is still distributed annually to the old folk of Shipton.

The church is an interesting one and possesses one of the sixty medieval stone pulpits which remain in the whole country. Unusual too, is the 'double-decker' tomb in the churchyard.

There are records that in 1845, the village post office was in the hands of the great-great-grandfather of the present postmistress. Surely few small villages can boast not only a continuity of the premises but also the family, as postmasters, over such a long period.

BURFORD

Here is another town that was an important centre of the wool trade and in the seventeenth century famous not only for the stone that was quarried nearby, but also for its master craftsmen. Sir Christopher Wren recommended that one, Christopher Kempster, a Burford man, should be employed on the building of St Paul's and he became Wren's clerk of works. Kempster owned Kitts Quarries at Upton.

Today, Burford prides itself on being a 'gateway' to the Cotswolds, and it is indeed a very good centre. There is much of interest locally and many of the old inns remain. Certainly this is a town in which to wander and explore.

The church is quite fascinating, with its chantry chapels and the elaborate tomb of Sir Lawrence Tanfield, Lord Chief Baron of the Exchequer, to two monarchs, Elizabeth and James I. Another monument is to the memory of Harman Sylvester, who served as barber to Henry VIII and was one of the witnesses to his will.

SWINBROOK

This is a large village with its houses scattered about the hillside, and was once the property of the Fettiplace family.

The church is 700 years old and though only small, manages to encompass within its walls a number of monuments of the former lords of the manor. Interesting is the way in which space has been conserved, for the deceased Fettiplace's are arranged as it were on shelves, one above the other. The three Tudor gentlemen lie with their elbows on cushions, heads in hands and fully attired in armour. Uncomfortable they may be but no one would guess it from their studied nonchalance.

MINSTER LOVELL

This beautiful and historic village is tucked away off the main road to Oxford about five miles from Burford. Here is a sample of real old England: the fifteenth century bridge spanning the river Windrush, the village street with an abundance of thatched cottages and at the end of it the 500-year-old church. As if this is not enough, close by is the impressive ruin of the old manor house, with which is associated a grim and tragic story.

It concerns the 13th Lord Lovell who escaped from the battle of Stoke, where he had been supporting Lambert Simnell. After the defeat he swam his horse across the river Trent and eventually arriving at the house, hid with the connivance of a trusted servant in a secret room. The man was the only one who knew of his Lordship's arrival and he cared for him for some days. Then he met with an accident and Lord Lovell cooped up in his secret room died of starvation. During repairs to the house early in the eighteenth century, the chamber was discovered and in it was found the skeleton of a man seated at a table, with the skeleton of a faithful hound at his feet. Positive identification was never made but neither was Lord Lovell ever heard of again.

The church is quite remarkable for the four piers which carry the tower, and there is a very fine fifteenth century tomb of the Lovell who built the church.

FILKINS

This attractive little village is on the Burford to Swindon road, and certainly its graceful main street was never meant for twentieth century traffic.

Here is a unique folk museum, which has been brought into being by one man and is housed in two diminutive sixteenth century cottages. Beside one of them is the old lock-up. Its occupants were rarely guilty of a worse crime than imbibing too freely, and a night in the cramped, airless accommodation must have indeed been punishment enough.

The museum with its display of household implements of days gone by, is quite fascinating.

The modern village centre was built and presented to the inhabitants by the late Sir Stafford and Lady Cripps.

GREAT BARRINGTON

The village of Great Barrington and Barrington Park make an attractive pair. For at least 300 years deer have roamed in the park and, close to the road there is a portion of the wall with a sunken fence designed to enable any stray deer to regain access to the park. It also serves to give passers-by a fine view of the herd, if it happens to be grazing on that side.

Two memorials make the church famous. One, sculptured in marble is accepted as being one of the finest in England, and represents two of the Bray children from the family who until

1734 lived at the great mansion in the park. The memorial depicts two children, Jane aged eight, who died in 1711 and Edward who died in 1720 aged fifteen. The boy, dressed in a square braided coat, holds his young sister by the hand. His eyes are fixed on an escorting guardian angel, whose protecting wings overshadow the children. The girl is half turned to look back as they walk among the clouds of heaven. They were two of a family of ten who died of smallpox, the little boy on Christmas day. The memorial is believed to be the work of Francis Bird, who executed some of the work in St Paul's Cathedral.

In the north aisle, almost hidden by the organ, is the interesting tomb of Captain Edmund Bray. Clad in Tudor armour, he is wearing his sword on the right side instead of the left: the reason being that he killed a man at Tilbury camp but was pardoned by Queen Elizabeth, whereupon he vowed never again to draw his sword with his right hand.

EASTLEACH TURVILLE AND EASTLEACH MARTIN

These delightful twin villages aided by a fine old clapper bridge, melt gracefully into one. Even so, there is an ancient church each side of the shallow river Leach, which divides what were for centuries, two distinct villages and two parishes.

Eastleach Turville on the east bank rises up the hillside and has some pleasing houses and rows of cottages looking over a sylvan scene. Turville is the name of the family who owned the land on that side of the river long ago. The clapper bridge which alone joined the two until the road bridge was built, was erected by John Keble, the divine and poet who for eight years was in charge of the two parishes.

Eastleach Turville church was once served by monks from an abbey near Chipping Norton. Recently some minor repairs to the north wall led to the interesting discovery. Two pillars, one with a carved head the other with a ball motif were found tight to the existing wall, showing that in earlier days the church extended well beyond its present limits in that direction.

Eastleach Martin church, a stone's throw across the stream, was built towards the end of the eleventh century but it is not so attractive as its twin. The founder was one of five Norman brothers, who followed William the Conqueror. Later the founder bestowed it on Malvern Priory "for the good of hys soule", and the deed of gift is still to be seen in the British Museum.

It is only in the last twenty years or so that the two parishes have been civilly united. Both churches are maintained and services are held in one or the other each Sunday.

The Eastleach villages are not as well known as others in the Cotswolds, but they are a delight and well worth visiting.

FAIRFORD'S GLORIOUS CHURCH

An early English church stood on the site of the present building which, with the exception of the tower, was demolished towards the end of the fifteenth century. The rebuilding was the gift of a prosperous wool stapler, John Tame, who lived at Fairford in 1470, and is buried in the north chapel. His son, Edmund Tame, carried on his father's good works and also has a memorial in the Lady Chapel. He died in 1534.

The church, a perfect example of the Perpendicular period, is justly famous for its magnificent windows dated 1500, and the misericord seats in the choir. The timber roof has sixty-nine angels to help support it.

The beautiful windows are judged to contain some of the best fifteenth century glass in England. There are twenty-eight of them and it is amazing that they have survived the excursions and alarms of more than 400 years. Only one group, the Judgment scenes of the great west window, has sustained damage which was caused by a storm in 1703. The window is astounding in its size, scope and execution. We can only wonder at the skill and imagination of the master craftsmen who were responsible. The scene which depicts the last day, when the graves give up their dead and St Michael weighs them in the balance deciding which shall pass to eternal life or which are doomed to destruction with Satan in hell, is quite fantastic in its detail.

It was fortunate that the windows escaped the troubles and religious strife of the reigns of Elizabeth, James and Cromwell, and it is thought that they were removed and buried for safety at least during the Civil war. This happened again in 1940, when they were stored in the cellars of Fairford Park, a mansion now demolished.

The windows of Fairford church portray hundreds of characters – the twelve apostles, the saints, including Sebastian tied to a tree, Pilate, Roman soldiers, David pronouncing judgment on the Amalekite, Solomon giving judgment, St Michael in golden armour, etc. They are rich, beautiful and contain scores of visual scriptural incidents. Many stories have been told about them. They were said in the first place to have been part of a cargo of a captured ship, but there are many pointers that they are of Flemish design, though made in England by English craftsmen. To support this theory there are many similarities in the windows of King's College, Cambridge, which are known to have been the work of Englishmen. It is now believed that they were all the work of Bernard Flower, the king's glazier, a Fleming, who directed English workmen at Westminster.

A reason advanced for their miraculous escape from

destruction during religious strife was that they were taken out and refitted *upside down*, thus forming a mosaic rather than a picture. When they were re-leaded in 1889, pieces were discovered to be upside down and the windows generally had obviously been reset by unskilled workmen. Even so, it is hardly likely that the zealous cohorts of Cromwell would have been fooled by such a device.

The misericord seats in the choir were also the work of master craftsmen, who brought both their imagination and sense of humour into play. The carving of the seats depict everyday scenes of the life of the times. A fox destroying ducks; a woman cooking over a fire and a dog stealing food from a pot; a man and woman drinking from a barrel, are typical of the scenes on the fourteen seats.

Misericords, as the name implies, were seats of pity or compassion, provided to give support to the older clergy who were taking part in lengthy services. They were tip-up seats so constructed that they could be used in the ordinary way, or when tipped up, provided a broad ledge which would give a fair measure of support to anyone leaning against them. It was the underside of the ledge that was invariably beautifully carved.

KEMPSFORD

Kempsford off the Cirencester/Fairford road is a village which saw some of the eighteenth century history of the Thames and Severn canal. Construction began in 1783, with the object of effecting a connection between the rivers Severn and Thames. It was a gigantic engineering feat, which cost a quarter of a million pounds. From Stroud Water canal it rose by a series of twenty-eight locks to the height of 240 feet. It then entered a 'legging tunnel' 2¼ miles in length, followed by a seven-mile uninterrupted 'cut'. Then it descended to Lechlade by sixteen locks. The venture never paid its way and it was finally abandoned in 1911.* One can see traces of the dried-up bed of the waterway at Kempsford for a humped-back bridge is always a sure sign of a canal in the vicinity.

The church, however, is the showpiece of the village. Its crowning glory is the wonderful tower built by John of Gaunt in 1390, in memory of his first wife, Lady Blanche Plantagenet, the mother of King Henry IV. The building is a history book in stone, illustrating architecture from the Norman period to the mid-fifteenth century.

For hundreds of years Kempsford was closely associated with kings and the greatest families in the land. In 1761, however, a notorious family purchased the manor. Gabriel Hanger, later created Baron Coleraine in the Irish peerage, was lord of the manor for twelve years until his death. Then his son succeeded to the title, but he died in Paris in 1794. The estate then passed to a brother, William, who was one of the 'rakes' of the Regency period and an associate of the fops who surrounded the Prince Regent. Known as 'old Blue Hanger' from an attachment he once showed for a blue coat, he had lived much of his life at the French court and affected the exaggerated manners of that period. He died in 1814, aged seventy years, and was buried in Kempsford church.

The next of this dreadful family was George, known as 'Blue Hanger', but he never accepted the title, so that on his death it became extinct. This man was by far and away the worst of the bunch. He spent most of his youth at Eton making love to tradesmen's daughters, then he married a gypsy, who later eloped with a tinker. 'Blue Hanger' served in the Dragoons during the American war and was also a boon companion of the Prince Regent. His extravagance was notorious and he was

*The story of the canal is told in *Cotswold Countryside and its Characters*.

eventually committed to prison for debt. On his release he set up in business as a coal merchant. In his lifetime he maintained that if he was buried underground the devil would get him more quickly, so evil had his life been. When he died in 1824, his white marble coffin was set on a pedestal 4 ft from the ground in the south chapel. The chapel, however, was rebuilt in 1858, and the opportunity was taken to place the coffin under the organ with the top at floor level. In his life he had many unsavoury distinctions; in his death, he had the doubtful distinction of being the only Irish Peer to be buried beneath an organ in an English church.

DOUBLES AND TREBLES

There are a number of Cotswold villages bearing the same main name and in most cases such villages, although close to each other, each have their own church.

Coln St. Aldwyns	Great Rissington
Coln St. Dennis	Little Rissington
Coln Rogers	Wyck Rissington

The pairs consist of:—

Great Barrington	Eastleach Martin	Shipton Oliffe
Little Barrington	Eastleach Turville	Shipton Sollars
Temple Guiting	Lower Slaughter	Lower Swell
Guiting Power	Upper Slaughter	Upper Swell

North Cerney and South Cerney

There are four villages of Duntisbourne and of Ampney:

Duntisbourne Abbots	Ampney Crucis
Duntisbourne Rouse	Ampney St. Mary
Middle Duntisbourne	Ampney St. Peter
Duntisbourne Leer	Down Ampney

(Only two have churches).

HISTORIC CHURCHES' PRESERVATION TRUST

As has been mentioned in the foregoing pages, the parish church is usually the oldest building in almost every village and with the drift from the country to the towns, which has taken place over the last few decades, a great many former flourishing parishes now consist of a much diminished population.

It is quite unthinkable that these ancient churches should be allowed to fall into ruin, yet they must in many cases do so unless help and interest from outside the parish is forthcoming. This great problem led to the formation in 1952, of a non-denominational Trust with the object of providing grants to supplement the efforts of parishes to maintain many of these architectural and historical 'gems'.

Fine work has already been accomplished, for more than a thousand churches and chapels in every part of the country have been assisted by either grants or interest-free loans, but a large amount is still needed if this worthy object is to be continued.

All lovers of ancient churches can obtain details of the Trust's work, and donations may be sent to the Historic Churches' Preservation Fund, Fulham Palace, London, S.W.6.

INDEX

Bold figures denote illustrations

OTHER BRIEF GUIDES

1.	EXMOOR COUNTRY	2s 6d
2.	COTSWOLD COUNTRY	2s 6d
3.	RALEIGH COUNTRY	2s 6d
4.	TORBAY AREA	2s 6d
5.	CORNWALL & ISLES OF SCILLY	2s 6d
7.	ANCIENT CHURCHES	2s 6d
8.	OXFORD'S COUNTRY	2s
10.	INN SIGNS	2s
11.	ISLE OF WIGHT & NEW FOREST	2s
12.	MORE ABOUT INN SIGNS	2s
13.	HARDY COUNTRY OF DORSET	2s
18.	YORKSHIRE	2s
19.	SHAKESPEARE COUNTRY	2s
20.	LAKE DISTRICT	2s 6d
21.	THE MOTORIST'S COUNTRYSIDE	2s
22.	CANALS & WATERWAYS	2s 6d
23.	THE SEVERN & ITS BORE	2s 6d
24.	NORTH WALES	2s
25.	DARTMOOR	2s 6d